P9-CRA-177

ON

WITTGENSTEIN

Jaakko Hintikka
Boston University

Wadsworth
Thomson Learning.

Australia • Canada • Mexico • Singapore • Spain
United Kingdom • United States

Printed in the United States of America
1 2 3 4 5 6 7 03 02 01 00 99

For permission to use material from this text, contact us:
Web: http://www.thomsonrights.com
Fax: 1-800-730-2215
Phone: 1-800-730-2214

For more information, contact:
Wadsworth/Thomson Learning, Inc.
10 Davis Drive
Belmont, CA 94002-3098
USA
http://www.wadsworth.com

ISBN: 0-534-57594-3

Table of Contents

PREFACE

After the Order of Merit was conferred on G.E. Moore by George VI in 1951, he responded to his wife with amazement: "Can you imagine - the King had not heard of Wittgenstein!" By the end of the century one's amazement would have been even greater. Ludwig Wittgenstein (1889-1951) is probably the most widely known philosopher of the twentieth century. An enormous number of books and papers have been written on him. "Wittgenstein" is one of the recognized categories of specialization in departments of philosophy in the United States. Yet the question may legitimately be raised whether Wittgenstein's thought has been understood half-way adequately. This question was raised, in effect, by Wittgenstein himself when he expressed the fear that the only heritage he would leave in philosophy is a certain jargon.

To what extent his fears have turned out to be justified is not for me to estimate here. It is indisputable in any case that attempts have been made to put his philosophy to the service of many causes which not only are not his own but which he would have found repugnant. It is therefore crucially important to try to understand what his thought is like in its own right and also to understand what Wittgenstein was like as a thinker. Wittgenstein himself rejected most traditional philosophical problems and ideas as nonsense and jokingly compared the intellectual and moral quality of the leading British philosophy journal *Mind* unfavorably with American pulp detective magazines. It is therefore ill-advised to discuss Wittgenstein by reference to the conventional philosophical ideas and problems, even though this is what is done in typical academic writings on Wittgenstein.

Preface

In the following pages I have tried to locate the most central ideas of Wittgenstein's at the different periods of his philosophical career and to trace their development. Much of what I will say may be like Wittgenstein's own philosophical ladder which should be thrown away after the reader has climbed up through it. However, I do believe that such an exercise is needed in order to see Wittgenstein's world aright.

Needless to say, in writing this book I have made use of a wide variety of sources and other material, a greater variety than I can here acknowledge. Three debts are nevertheless too great to go unmentioned. They are to G. H. von Wright who first introduced me to Wittgenstein's philosophy (and to Wittgenstein) and who in my judgment understands Wittgenstein more deeply than does anyone else. He also deserves, more than anyone else the credit of saving Wittgenstein's *Nachlass* for posterity and making it available to philosophers. Concerning the diagnosis and consequences of Wittgenstein's dyslexia I have profited from the expertise of Anna-Maija Hintikka. The third one is to the late Merrill Bristow Hintikka. Working with her on Wittgenstein was one of the most exciting intellectual adventures of my life. I hope that I can convey some of that excitement to my readers.

1

Who Was Ludwig Wittgenstein?

Who-questions can be asked for many different purposes and answered in different ways. A few such different construals of the title question and answers to them can serve as a composite portrait of Ludwig Wittgenstein.

One such question was in effect asked by the Austrian sculptor Michael Drobil. After the defeat of Austria in World War I, Ludwig Wittgenstein found himself in a dreary prisoners-of-war camp in Como, Italy. One day, he was chatting with a fellow prisoner named Michael Drobil. At one time, their conversation turned to the famous portrait by Klimt of Margarete Wittgenstein Stonborough.

> To Drobil's amazement, Wittgenstein referred to the painting as "the portrait of my sister." He stared in disbelief: "Then, you're a Wittgenstein are you?" (Monk. p 158)

The precise nature of Drobil's amazement requires a couple of explanations. First, for an authentic Viennese, it was for a long time the Wittgenstein family rather than any one of its members that was a familiar social and cultural landmark. When I came to know in the early sixties a finely cultivated Viennese lady scholar (not a philosopher) and told her of my interest in the great Austrian philosopher, her first question was the true Viennese one: "Is he a member of the Wittgenstein family?"

Drobil's surprise was in fact prompted by the wealth and social position of the Wittgenstein family. Ludwig Wittgenstein's father, Karl Wittgenstein, had amassed a fortune that was one of the largest in Europe. Drobil, who became Ludwig's friend, was surprised that a shabby fellow prisoner was in reality a scion of such a family. From the standpoint of Ludwig's later convictions, however, the family wealth became a curse. He came to believe in Tolstoyan ideals of simple life and poverty. Accordingly, he gave away his share of the family fortune, but not to the poor. Since poverty is a blessing, the poor might be corrupted by these moneys. Consistent as ever, he gave everything to people who were filthy rich anyway, namely to his sisters and brothers. Earlier, Ludwig Wittgenstein had given a large sum of money to a number of writers and artists, including Rilke, Trakl and Kokoschka.

If the family wealth does not open interesting perspectives on Wittgenstein's character and life, another family characteristics does. This characteristics is an enormous musical and artistic talent. One of Ludwig's brothers was Paul Wittgenstein, the pianist. By the time he tragically lost his right hand in World War I, he was so famous that Ravel wrote a concerto for the left hand specifically for him. One of Ludwig's sisters was a painter. But the most gifted was Hans Wittgenstein, who was a musical genius of the highest order but ended up committing suicide. Ludwig had an abundance of artistic talents. He was highly musical, he did some sculpting in Drobil's studio, and in 1926, he designed a house for his sister's family. This remarkable house, which shows the signs of the influence of Wittgenstein's friend, the famous architect Loos, is still an architectural landmark in Vienna.

Ludwig Wittgenstein's philosophy shows a remarkable sensitivity to conceptual issues which is not unlike artistic sensitivity. But being a member of the Wittgenstein family meant above anything else having exceptionally high standards of achievement and conduct. These standards were so high that they resulted in or at least contributed to the suicide of three of Ludwig's brothers. At first, some of the standards were imposed by Karl Wittgenstein on his sons whom he expected to continue his business ventures. It took two suicides to convince him that his sons had stronger ambitions of their own of a different kind.

Ludwig was largely spared parental pressures, partly because he was not considered as gifted as his brothers and partly because he was as first aiming at a practical career in engineering. But the internal pressures were nevertheless extremely high. The same rigorous standards characteristic of the rest of the Wittgenstein family were clearly in evidence in Ludwig, too, throughout his life. He was constantly engaged in self-observation and self-criticism also when his work is concerned. The first main question he addressed to Russell was whether his ideas about the foundations of mathematics were of any value. In his notebooks, he is often interspersing comments on the success or lack thereof of his own philosophical efforts.

Monk has spoken in connection with Ludwig Wittgenstein about "the duty of a genius." I doubt that Wittgenstein would have liked this pompous phrase. Another way of characterizing the same aspect of his character and his relation to his work is to speak of the ambition of a member of a gifted and competitive family. Yet "ambition" and "competition" do not convey the right nuance, either. Wittgensteinian ambition meant setting one's intellectual, artistic and external standards extremely high, and competitiveness meant holding others to the same high standards as oneself.

Ludwig Wittgenstein studied engineering in Berlin and Manchester. While doing so, he became fascinated by the philosophical problems of mathematics and immediately began to develop ideas of his own on the subject. After an inconclusive visit to Frege, Wittgenstein went to Cambridge in order to study with one of the other leading figures in logic and the philosophy of mathematics at the time, Bertrand Russell. Characteristically, Wittgenstein also hoped to find out whether the ideas he already had were any good.

Wittgenstein's arrival and the beginning of his relations to Bertrand Russell is one of the turning-points in twentieth century philosophy. Russell's "discovery" of Wittgenstein in 1911 can be compared with the discovery of the young mathematical genius Ramanujan by Russell's friend G. H. Hardy two years later. Hardy had to ask about the unknown Indian who had out of the blue mailed Hardy a manuscript full of amazing results: Who is Ramanujan? Genius or fraud? In a similar way, Russell had to ask of the intense "German" (as Russell initially thought of Wittgenstein) who arrived uninvited to work with him: Who is Wittgenstein? Genius or fool? Genius is easier to recognize conclusively in mathematics than in philosophy. Hardy needed only a few hours (plus the cooperation of his colleague

3

Littlewood) to be convinced of Ramanujan's genius. Russell was at first amused, puzzled, intrigued, and exasperated by the fanatically serious and intense alien. It took him months instead of Hardy's one evening to realize that his "German" visitor was indeed a philosopher of the highest quality. One thing that initially put Russell off was Wittgenstein's intellectual and personal intensity which was indeed frequently too much even for the intensive Russell, not to speak of others. But Russell was himself at this very time engaged in what probably was the most intensive and important philosophical activity of his life. Russell and Wittgenstein found themselves involved in the same philosophical enterprise and became allies in it. Russell came to realize that the very same intensity that had at first disturbed him in Wittgenstein was in fact a mark of dedication and intellectual depth. Russell and Wittgenstein came to respect each others' dedicated quest of clarity and truth, and in that role were at that time close to each other also personally. In Chapter 2, it will be seen how closely related Wittgenstein's famous little book *Tractatus Logico-Philosophicus* (1921, English translation in 1922) is to Russell's ideas. Although Wittgenstein was technically only a research student and younger than his famous friend, he gradually became the intellectual leader of the joint enterprise.

World War I put an end to this relationship. Wittgenstein served in the Austrian army and Russell defended the pacifist cause in England. By the time the war and its immediate aftermath were over, Wittgenstein had finished the *Tractatus*. Russell wrote a preface to it and helped to have it translated and published. However, Wittgenstein's now found that Russell no longer understood what he was trying to say. Not only was a cooperation impossible, the two were never again close to each other personally either. Meanwhile, Wittgenstein had undergone his Tolstoyan conversion and decided to seek simple life as an elementary school teacher in the Lower Austrian mountains. The experiment did not work out, even though Wittgenstein worked hard at it. His temperament, especially his tremendous impatience, made him less than ideally suited for the job. He returned to Vienna, designed his sister's villa, and was gradually drawn close to the famous Vienna Circle, a loosely organized group of philosophers, scientists, and mathematicians whose informal leader was Moritz Schlick.

In spite of differences of philosophical style and temperament and in spite of sometimes frayed personal relations, Wittgenstein's thought

4

was for a while very close to that of the Vienna Circle. Even his most important personal conflict bears witness to this philosophical closeness. What happened in 1932 was that Wittgenstein accused Carnap, one of the leading members of the Vienna Circle, if not of an outright plagiarism of his ideas, then at least of using them without acknowledgment and without permission. These accusations related both to Wittgenstein's new ideas he had expounded orally in Vienna and also to the ideas from the *Tractatus*.

Schlick's murder and the Nazi annexation of Austria put an end to the activities of the Vienna Circle and made it dangerous for Ludwig Wittgenstein to live there. Meanwhile, he had re-established a connection with Cambridge. His first arrival back in Cambridge, in January, 1929, was reported by J. M. Keynes (who had orchestrated the return) to his wife by writing:

Well, God has arrived. I met him on the 5:15 train.

Wittgenstein began to teach in 1930 and was made professor in 1939. He resigned in 1947 but kept on thinking and writing. He died in 1951 of cancer.

But it is not only in considering his biography that we must ask: Who was Ludwig Wittgenstein? This question arises also in reading Wittgenstein and in trying to understand him. For the purpose of understanding fully his thought, we have to understand what he was like, how his mind worked and what motivated him. In answering this question, recognizing the qualities that this man had inherited as a member of the Wittgenstein family goes a long way. However, there are further personal qualities that are also useful to keep in mind. One of them is Wittgenstein's impatience. He was so intensively concerned with finding a solution to his current problems and in articulating it that he often — perhaps one can even say usually — failed to make clear what his problems were. Wittgenstein rejected most traditional problems as nonsense, but that does not mean that this own thought was not problem-oriented. There probably has never been a philosopher for whom thinking was a harder struggle than for Wittgenstein. In the summer of 1949, when he was already ill, his doctor had forbidden Wittgenstein to get involved in philosophical discussion too often because it was taxing his physical strength so much.

Wittgenstein was also too impatient to explain the solution that he had earlier reached to his problems, dealing with them by a few hints. When Wittgenstein first explained his new conception of the name-

5

object relation in 1935 in the *Brown Book*, he devotes two full pages to the problem, complete with an explanation of what was wrong with his earlier views, concrete examples of relevant language-games, and so on. But when he returns to it in the *Philosophical Investigations* I, sec. 37, all that he says is in its entirety this:

> What is the relation between name and thing named? Well, what *is it*? Look at language game (2) or another one: there you can see what that relation can consist in.

Another character trait that seems to have influenced Wittgenstein's philosophical argumentation is a certain streak of suspicion that one can perhaps see in his argumentation. A characteristic turn of this argumentation is for Wittgenstein to envisage an objection to his views and then to defend them by refuting the objection. This lends his philosophical writings a dialectical character. One corollary to this fact is that readers of Wittgenstein's writings must be alert to the question of whether he is in any given passage expounding his own philosophy or objections to it.

Another psychological peculiarity of Wittgenstein is his dyslexia. He acknowledges himself that

> [m]y bad spelling in youth . . . is connected with the whole of the rest of my character (my weakness in study)

The nature of this affliction and its possible effects on Wittgenstein as a philosophical thinker and writer are nevertheless so subtle and so unexplored that we might be well advised to consign them to silence here. Yet some of these effects are unmistakable.

2
How to Read Wittgenstein

Wittgenstein's fascinating life and complex personality are the stuff grand historical novels are made of. In view of his distinctive personality, and with a side glance at his neighbor and contemporary Robert Musil, one of his biographers might very well have given Wittgenstein's life story the title *Der Mann mit Eigenschaften*. But do these properties help one to understand his philosophical ideas? In light of the available evidence, the only possible answer might seem to be negative. It is not very likely that any other philosophers have ever been conscripted to serve so many different causes as Wittgenstein or been interpreted as arbitrarily. But perhaps the fault does not lie only with the would-be interpreters. Wittgenstein's writings are in some objective sense hard to understand, at least at the first sight. Even their format is unusual. The *Tractatus* consists of hierarchically numbered propositions. There are seven major propositions, numbered 1-7. Propositions explaining, elaborating, or defending proposition numbered n are numbered n.1, n.2, ... and likewise for further decimals. There are no obvious arguments for any of the propositions, and the argumentative structure of the work — if any — is not obvious.

Wittgenstein's posthumously published books consist typically of short paragraphs, sometimes numbered by Wittgenstein himself, sometimes by the editors. There are no chapter or section headings.

There are no philosophical theses in the ordinary sense and little explicit argumentation. Wittgenstein says himself that he is not putting forward any philosophical doctrines but merely relieving himself and his readers of the confusions and mental cramps caused by

> Verhexung unseres Verstandes durch die Mittel unserer
> Sprache. (*Philosophical Investigations* I, I.c. 109, in English,
> "the bewitchment of our intelligence by means of language")

All this has often led to the notion that Wittgenstein is not dealing with any substantial problems nor offering any positive views, at least not in his later philosophy. He is merely practicing a kind of intellectual psychotherapy. It is also widely believed that there is no argumentative structure in his writings and that he on purpose chose an aphoristic mode of writing.

Such views are deeply misleading, however. Wittgenstein tried for years to articulate his ideas in the form of a progressive argument, only to find that he could not. In the preface to the first draft of the *Philosophical Investigations*, he described his efforts as follows:

> I wrote down all these ideas originally as *remarks* or brief
> paragraphs; frequently as longer sequences dealing with the
> same subject, frequently moving by jumps from one subject to
> another. — My purpose was to unite all this in due course of
> time in a book of whose form I formed different ideas at
> different times. What seemed to me essential was
> nevertheless that in it ideas would proceed from one subject to
> another in a well-ordered sequence.
> Some four years ago I made the first attempt at such a
> synthesis. The result was unsatisfactory, and I made further
> attempts; until finally (some years later) I reached the
> conviction that it was all in vain and that I had to give up all
> such attempts. It turned out that the best I could write were
> always going to remain only philosophical remarks and that
> my ideas were lamed as soon as I tried to force them, against
> their natural tendency, into one sole track.

Why the difficulty? Even though the subject still awaits an adequate analysis, it is hard not to attribute Wittgenstein's struggles to his dyslexia. He went himself as far as to say that "my bad spelling in youth . . . is connected with the rest of my character."

If so, it follows that Wittgenstein's method of philosophical exposition were not a deliberate choice of a literary genre or style but was forced on him by his dyslexia, which apparently made it extremely difficult for him to articulate verbally longer linguistic and other symbolic structures such as proofs and other arguments. The best he could do is to epitomize what for others would have been a structured argument in a single memorable comparison or metaphor.

Another reason for Wittgenstein's indirect mode of exposition is his belief that no semantics and no metatheory is as such literally expressible in language. Such matters can only be explained through hints, clues and indirect explanation. Already in the *Tractatus*, Wittgenstein had declared in its penultimate proposition that what he had said there cannot be expressed by literally expressed propositions:

> My propositions are elucidatory in this way: he who
> understands one finally recognizes them as senseless, when he
> has climbed out through them, on them, over them. (He has
> so to speak throw away the ladder after he has climbed up on
> it.) He must surmount these propositions; then he will see the
> world rightly. (6.54)

This Wittgensteinian conviction will be discussed further below. It was not a peculiarity of Wittgenstein's, but a philosophical thesis (or perhaps rather a presupposition) that has played an extremely important role in twentieth-century philosophy in general.

In any case, a dyslexic's inability to articulate a structure, for instance an argumentative structure, verbally does not mean that he cannot master it in some other medium, for instance geometrically. It is therefore revealing that Wittgenstein should have preferred geometrical reasoning to logical and algebraic one. He went as far as to say that

> the logical certainty of proofs — I want to say — does not
> extend beyond their geometrical certainty. (*Remarks on the
> Foundation of Mathematics* III, sec. 43)

Thus there is no reason to believe that Wittgenstein's writings — at least those he hoped to develop into a book — do not have an argumentative structure, including conscious cross-references. Indeed, the contrary is clearly the case. At one point, Wittgenstein expressed to his friend and successor in Cambridge, G. H. von Wright, the metaphoric wish that his writings could be printed like an old-fashioned family Bible where after every verse there are cross-references to other parts of the Bible. Still less does it follow that

Wittgenstein did not deal with problems, albeit not traditional philosophical problems, or that he did not offer rational solutions to them.

But how can one find these solutions and the other constructive ideas Wittgenstein had found? Here a clue is offered by his method of working from the early thirties on. Wittgenstein wrote down his new philosophical ideas in a series of almost daily notebooks. These were the invaluable materials for his further work. He preserved them carefully. He put them in safes or left with friends and relatives for safekeeping. He even made copies of them to be on the safe side. When he felt that he had reached an overview, he hired a typist and dictated, partly from his notebooks and partly *ex tempore*, a book-length typescript which he hoped to develop into a publishable work. With the exception of Part I of *Philosophical Investigations*, he nevertheless ended up frustrated in these editorial efforts, and began the process anew. Now a normal person would find it very difficult to dictate sentence by sentence an extended discursive argument, let alone a book-length one, and for a dyslexic like Wittgenstein such an attempt must have been totally hopeless. What I would do and what I expect that the reader would do is to outline the leading ideas of the works in the first page or the first two-five-ten-twenty pages, storing it as it were in my long term memory. Then I could use this theory sketch as an Archimedean fixed point, offer reasons for it, defend it by imagining objections in order to refute them, enhance its readability by applying it to different problems to solve them, and above all to fill in the sketch in different ways. This is what Wittgenstein typically did, both in his book-length works and often also in his shorter arguments. Accordingly, the way one should read Wittgenstein is to focus on the beginning of the work or section of the work in question. A careful reading of the early pages will show the general picture he was painting or, rather, a sketch of its main features. The rest of the work has to be read with the main ideas revealed by the outline firmly in mind, always asking how what Wittgenstein says fits into the larger picture.

Of course, as every good recipe, this instruction needs to be implemented by a pinch of salt. For instance, Wittgenstein never intended the materials which are included as part II of the *Philosophical Investigations* to be published together with Part I. In one long typescript (TS 213 von Wright), Wittgenstein made an effort to compose an ordinary book, complete with chapters and chapter titles as well as sections and section titles. The result did not satisfy him in the end, however, and the conventional format does not help to understand Wittgenstein's argumentation much better than his usual loose one.

Taking a clue from these insights, it will be shown in the subsequent chapters how Wittgenstein's thought and its development can be understood. Contrary to widespread misconceptions, Wittgenstein turns out to have held definite logico-philosophical views at the different stages of his career. Furthermore, his philosophical development does not involve quantum jumps from one grand thesis or one philosophical method to another. Rather, typically, Wittgenstein's earlier views led to problems whose solution necessitated positive changes in his ideas about logic, language, and philosophy. Indeed, it is not too much of an exaggeration to say that the story of Wittgenstein's philosophical development is like a good mystery story. Once you have finished it, you have the feeling that you should have seen the *dénouement* much earlier.

3

A Russellian Tract Entitled
Tractatus

What happens if these hermeneutical principles are applied to Wittgenstein's *Tractatus Logico-Philosophicus*? Even though this work was composed by Wittgenstein in a way different from his later writings and even though it in a sense constitutes one long — or not so long — argument, the overall structure matches the expositorial paradigm explained above. Wittgenstein begins by sketching a general view of the structure of the world, language, and thought, including their relations to each other. Some of the main propositions are as follows:

1	The world is everything that is the case.
1.1	The world is the totality of facts, not of things.
2	What is the case, the fact, is the existence of atomic facts.
2.1	An atomic fact is a combination of objects (entities, things).
2.0123	If I know an object, then I also know all the possibilities of its occurring in atomic facts.

2.022	It is clear that however different from the real one an imagined world may be, it must have something — a form — in common with the real world.
2.023	This fixed form consists of the objects.
2.061	Atomic facts are independent of each other.
2.1	We make ourselves pictures of facts.
2.12	The picture is a model of reality.
2.1514	The representing relation consists of due coordinations of the elements of the picture and the things.
2.2	The picture has the logical form of representation in common with what it pictures.
3	The logical picture of the facts is the thought.

And so on. It does not take a skeptical reader to ask: How does Wittgenstein know all this? Where do all these sweeping theses come from? For instance, how does Wittgenstein know that the structure of the world consists of unanalyzable objects combined into atomic facts?

The first glimpse of the historical background of the *Tractatus* provides an answer. The most important feature of this background in pre-World-War-I Cambridge was Bertrand Russell's theory of knowledge by acquaintance which he had arrived at after a number of experiments with several different philosophical theories and several changes of mind. The most important background assumption of Russell's theory was in turn the realistic thesis of G. E. Moore to the effect that every experience is an experience of something. In other, more explicit words, in each experience, we can according to Moore distinguish the immediate object from the experience as a mere psychological event. That object is given to me; I am directly aware of it.

These direct objects of experience became in Russell's thought — and in his terminology — the objects of acquaintance. For instance, in perceptual experience, I can distinguish the object of perception from the perception as a psychological event. However, these direct objects of perception are not ordinary physical objects, for our perceptions of ordinary objects can be mistaken. They were called by Russell sense-data. Russell insisted that sense-data are part of the physical world, but never explained fully what they are. Besides particular objects, we can according to Russell have acquaintance with universals, apparently

13

entities of any logical type in the sense of Russell's and Whitehead's *Principia Mathematica*. Other candidates are considered below. According to Russell, the objects of acquaintance are all that is given to us. All our knowledge and all our concepts must be based on them. The object which we are not immediately "acquainted" with, Russell called objects of description. They must be reducible to objects of acquaintance (this was Russell's famous "reduction to acquaintance"). In our usual thinking, we take them to be inferred from experience. Russell wanted to consider them as logical constructs from objects of acquaintance. As he puts it, he wanted to replace inferences to unknown entities by logical constructions. Every proposition must thus be analyzable into objects of acquaintance. Objects of acquaintance are the end points of this analysis. They cannot be analyzed any further; they are simple. Because of their status as the end-points of all analysis, objects of acquaintance cannot themselves be described any longer. We cannot define them or even say that they exist, for that would presuppose that we can analyze them further.

In such works as *Our Knowledge of the External World* (1914), Russell gives guidelines and some sketchy examples as to how the reduction to acquaintance can be carried out.

This is the obvious precedent of the structure of the Tractarian world which can be analyzed into simple objects. Only a thinker who is only standing on Russell's shoulders — or, rather, on the shoulders of Russell's theory of acquaintance — can have the chutzpah of putting forward the similar theory we find in the *Tractatus* without much overt evidence or argument. Wittgenstein's *Tractatus* is in the simplest possible terms a variation of the Russellian theory of acquaintance.

From this perspective, we can already appreciate several of the most central features of the *Tractatus*. Wittgenstein's world there was a phenomenological one. His objects were like Russell's objects of acquaintance. They were the objects of my experiences. As his best early interpreter once put it,

> Wittgenstein says it is nonsense to believe in anything not given in experience. . . . For to be mine, to be given in experience, is the formal [definitory] property to be a genuine entity. (From item # 004-21-02 of the Ramsey archives of Pittsburgh.)

One nevertheless has to watch one's terminology here. Phenomenology is so often confused even by well-informed philosophers with phenomenalism. A phenomenologist maintains that the rock bottom of my world epistemologically and conceptually is what is given to one in immediate experience. This leaves open the question as to what it is that is given to one in immediate experience. A phenomenalist answers this question by saying that we have direct access only to the contents of our consciousness, phenomena rather than things themselves. Even though the history of these terms is somewhat murky, it is clear that Wittgenstein was never a phenomenalist, although there is a sense in which it can perhaps be said of Wittgenstein's philosophy that it is a "phenomenology."

Wittgenstein made it clear, in any case, that the objects postulated in the *Tractatus* included such phenomenological entities as colors and points in my visual space. However this does not mean that these objects are mere phenomena, any more than Russellian sense-data are mere appearances. Perhaps the best way of describing Wittgenstein's objects is to say that they are indeed ingredients of physical reality in so far as they are objects of any immediate experience.

Instead of documenting the phenomenological character of Wittgenstein's simple objects in the *Tractatus*, it is more instructive to indicate how it throws light on some of the most perplexing passages of the *Tractatus*. In 6.43, Wittgenstein writes:

> The world of the happy is quite another than that of the unhappy.

Where does this mystical-sounding view come from? The right answer is: G. E. Moore. A happy person is the one who enjoys the most valuable "unmixed goods." According to Moore, they include such experiences as the pleasures of personal experience and the contemplation of beautiful objects. But what happens if another person — an unhappy one — does not have the same experience, for instance, does not perceive the same objects as beautiful as I do? Moore answers firmly, true to his realist doctrine of the objects of experience, that such a person literally perceives a different object. If we simply add to these Moorean conclusions the Wittgensteinian idea that the objects that constitute the substance of my world are the object of my experience, we must conclude literally that the unhappy philistine has different objects in his world than my objects of experience. Thus, Wittgenstein's puzzling thesis becomes merely an inevitable conclusion from Moore's Bloomsbury ethic.

This is confirmed by the rest of section 6.43 of *Tractatus* which shows that for Wittgenstein, the worlds of a happy and an unhappy man have different limits, that is, different objects. If there is a difference between Moore and Wittgenstein, it is that for Wittgenstein, values were revealed by experiences of willing rather than experiences of different kinds of enjoyment:

> If good or bad willing changes the world, it can only change the limits of the world, not the facts. . . . In brief, our world must thereby become quite another. It must so to speak wax or wane on a whole.

Hence, the ontology and the semantics of the *Tractatus* are by and large analogous to Russell's. The world is a world of simple objects which are phenomenological in the sense of being objects of my immediate experience. Everything else can be considered as so many logical constructs from the simple objects. All we can talk about are these objects. Hence, they must be given to one in order for one to say anything or think anything, and anything I can think of or speak of is a construction of these objects. Furthermore, the parallelism between Russell and Wittgenstein implies that for Wittgenstein, too, properties and relations are also objects, not only particulars.

A simple object is represented in language by a name. These can be combined in the same way as the objects they represent. The sentence in which they are combined in a certain way expresses the proposition that their objects are related to each other in a corresponding manner.

But how are such name-object relations set up? And how can we refer to the simple objects in a way that does not already presuppose their existence? Wittgenstein does not answer these questions in the *Tractatus*, but Russell has answered it for them — and for himself. According to Russell, these are only "logically proper names" in English, that is, truly presuppositionless ways of referring to objects of acquaintance, viz. "this," "that", and "I." Wittgenstein denies the ego, the reference of "I," the status of a simple object, and hence denies that "I" names an object. But for Wittgenstein, too, there is a inseparable tie between the idea of object and such ostensive pointing as is signaled by "this" and "that."

> We seem to be given as *a priori* the concept: *This*. — Identical with the concept of the *object*. (*Notebooks 1914-16*, p. 61)

But — as was seen — of the simple objects we cannot say that they exist or define them (because then one could say that the definendum exists). Hence, they can be instantiated only by pointing to them and uttering "This" or "That." We do not say what they are, we show them. This explains one of the most puzzling features of the *Tractatus*. It is Wittgenstein's contrast between what can be said and what can only be shown. This contrast is connected with, and can be considered as a consequence of, a deep-seated belief by Wittgenstein in the inexpressibility of all meaning relations. Since they come down to knowing the simple, unanalyzable objects, there is nothing we can say of these simples. We can only point to them and say "this" or "that." We can only show them. Hence Wittgenstein's saying-showing terminology is to be understood almost literally.

4

Wittgenstein's Picture Theory

But there is also a major difference between Russell and Wittgenstein. Russell's theory of acquaintance was supposed to explain, not only the structure of our knowledge, but also the structure of propositions, including the conditions on their meaningfulness. What is for instance required if I am to understand a simple (elementary) relational proposition of the form R(a,b), for instance, "Ludwig hits Karl," assuming that it is fully analyzed? In order to understand this proposition, I have to be acquainted with its simplest ingredients, in this case Ludwig, Karl, and the relation of hitting. But this is not enough. In order to understand R(a,b), I must for instance distinguish it from the converse proposition R(b,a), in the example "Karl hits Ludwig." Since the two involve the same three objects of acquaintance, something else is needed. This something else is according to Russell the logical form of the proposition in question. All basic ingredients of a proposition, it must also be an object of acquaintance. Likewise, there must be logical forms characteristic of various structures of propositions, such as disjunction and conjunction.

18

These objects are called "logical objects" and their representation in language "logical constants." Thus, Russell postulated a separate class of objects of acquaintance called "logical forms."

Russell explained this culmination of his theory of acquaintance in the book *Theory of Knowledge* which he wrote in 1913. He made the mistake of showing it to Wittgenstein who was highly critical, not to say contemptuous, telling Russell that he had himself entertained similar ideas but found them entirely wrong. Russell was so discouraged that he never published the entire *Theory of Knowledge*. It appeared posthumously in 1984 as volume 7 of Russell's *Collected Papers*.

This pinpoints Wittgenstein's *Tractatus* precisely in relation to Russell. The *Tractatus* is nothing more and nothing less than Russell's 1913 theory *sans* logical forms as objects of acquaintance. This relationship was for a long time obscured by philosophers' unawareness of Russell's for a long time unpublished book. Wittgenstein himself was nevertheless fully aware of the relation:

> My fundamental thoughts is that "logical constants" do not represent [anything]. (*Tractatus* 4.0312)

> Here it becomes clear that there are no such things as "logical objects" or "logical constants" (in the sense of Frege and Russell). (*Tractatus* 5.4)

But the rejection of logical objects thrust on Wittgenstein the task of explaining structural meaning without them. If a proposition is not held together by the "logical glue" provided by logical forms as actually existing objects of acquaintance, what does hold it together? Wittgenstein's answer was: A proposition is held together, not by any additional "tie" or "glue" but by the forms of its constituents. Objects are connected with each other in a proposition, not like tiles cemented together, but like jigsaw-puzzle pieces held in place by their form.

In a proposition objects hang together like links in a chain.

More literally speaking,

> The logical form of the proposition must already be given by the forms of the component parts. (*Notebooks* 1914-16, p. 23)

This is Wittgenstein's famous "picture theory of language." Its gist is readily explained, not by trying to spell out directly how propositions can be interpreted as pictures, but how a picture can have a propositional content. Suppose I try to convey to you the message

"Ludwig hits Karl" by showing you a picture of the two *in flagrante delicto*. What is it you have to gasp in order to get the point? Many details are undoubtedly unnecessary. What is needed is, first, enough detail to enable you to recognize the antagonists as Ludwig and Karl, respectively. But you do not have to convey this information by a mass of detail. It can be done by attaching the name labels "Ludwig" and "Karl" to the two figures in the picture and perhaps eventually replacing these figures by their names. Likewise the only additional thing you need to do is to recognize the goings-on in the picture as hitting. This can also be done by placing the word label "hits" between the two figures and omitting everything else as irrelevant. In this way, the telltale picture can be transformed into the sentence "Ludwig hits Karl" without losing any features of the picture that are needed to convey the intended message. In this sense, the picture and the sentence are completely on a par. You can view the proposition (sentence) as a picture, or the picture as a proposition.

This "picture theory" helps the reader to understand the propositions quoted above from the *Tractatus*. At the same time, these propositions conversely will help you to understand what has just been said.

This so-called "picture theory" of language is a simple but at the same time instructive model as to how language works. According to this model, simple objects are represented in language by names. By combining the names in a certain way, one can express the proposition that the objects named are related to each other in the corresponding way. For instance, the fact that the names "Karl," "Ludwig" are combined with the name (in a wide sense of the term) "hits" or in the sentence "Ludwig hits Karl" says that the objects named are similarly related, or, in other words, that Ludwig hits Karl. The requirement that a name must always have the same logical form as its object guarantees that the totality of all possible combinations of objects matches the totality of all possible combinations of names. A proposition is true if and only if the objects are in fact related to each other in the same way as the names in the proposition.

It follows that the world (the actual world) is characterized by the totality of facts about it (cf. *Tractatus* 1-1.11). This totality is determined not by the totality of objects, for objects could be combined with each other in other ways too, so it is the form of propositions that corresponds to every possible state of affairs. Indeed, the same objects can occur also in other possible states of affairs.

The totality of ways in which a simple object can be combined with others is determined by its logical form. Thus, the logical forms of simple objects do the same job for Wittgenstein as the free-standing logical forms were supposed to do for Russell. But unlike Russellian logical forms (of the 1913 vintage), they cannot be separated from the objects whose forms they are. Since the logical forms of simple objects are the ultimate constituents of all logical forms, the structure of logic according to *Tractatus* is radically different from most other conceptions of logic. Usually, logic is taken to deal with the most general features of the world. According to Wittgenstein, logic is grounded on the most specific features of the world, the simple objects.

Moreover, simple logical forms are given together with the objects whose forms they are. Since these objects are the objects of my immediate experience, their forms are also phenomenological. Accordingly, any analysis of the logical structure of the world and the logical structure underlying our language must in the last analysis be phenomenological in nature. Logic or — to use Wittgenstein's euphemism, grammar — is thus assimilated by him to phenomenology. "Phenomenology is grammar," he writes repeatedly.

The picture theory of the *Tractatus* looks like a marvelous model as to how an ideal language can be thought of as operating. It explains both the mechanism of meaning and the conditions of truth. But are there any reasons for believing that this is how our language actually works? The picture theory is eminently plausible as applied to the simplest propositions (a.k.a. elementary or atomic propositions). But how can it be extended to all complex ones? Wittgenstein was painfully aware that it is humanly impossible to gather immediately the logic of our colloquial language which "is a part of the human organism and not less complicated than it" (*Tractatus* 4.002). In order to avoid serious problems,

> we must employ a symbolism which excludes them. . . . A symbolism that is to say, that obeys the rules of *logical* grammar — of logical syntax. (3.325)

But where do we find such a perfect symbolism? In Wittgenstein's historical context, the answer is obvious. The symbolism of Russell's and Whitehead's *Principia Mathematica* was calculated to be such a *lingua universalis*. Indeed, Wittgenstein continues the quoted passage as follows:

21

The logical symbolism of Frege and Russell is such a
language, which, however, does not exclude all errors.

The "errors" which Wittgenstein found (or thought he had found)
in the *Principia* need not detain us here. They do not reflect on the
near-identity of the symbolism of the *Principia* with a language
"governed by the rules of logical grammar."

Now what is a Frege-Russell language like? It is a language
which relies essentially on propositional connectives and quantifiers (of
any logical type). Hence, Wittgenstein's problem becomes: How can
we construct such a quantificational language so as to be able to
interpret all its propositions as pictures?

Wittgenstein thought that he could deal with quantified
propositions by considering them as maximal disjunctions and
conjunctions. Thus, an existentially quantified proposition $(\exists x)S[x]$ is
logically equivalent with the disjunction

$S[a] \vee S[b] \vee \ldots.$

where a, b, ... are all the different objects of the appropriate
logical form. However, in order for the disjunction to be logically
equivalent with $(\exists x)\ S[x]$, the two must be interchangeable in every
possible situation, i.e., in every "possible world." But that is possible
only if all the individuals a, b, ... exist in all possible situations and if
these objects are all the individuals existing in each of them. In brief,
all the objects I have must apparently exist necessarily, and they must
exhaust all existing objects.

This sounds highly implausible. Where could Wittgenstein have
possibly thought that he can find such a class of necessary objects?
The answer is implicit in what has already been said. Tractarian simple
objects are the Russellian objects of acquaintance. They are all the
objects of my experience. And it is this experience of mine to which I
must be able to reduce everything. Simple objects are the end points of
this reduction. As Russell already pointed out in *Theory of Knowledge*,
this means that it is impossible to say anything of these basic objects,
just because everything must be understood by reference to them.

Hence, I cannot say anything (at least not in a literal sense) about
a simple object, not even that it exists, or that it does not exist.
Because the objects are in this sense transcendental, I have to deal with
my objects of acquaintance as if they existed necessarily and together
necessarily exhausted everything that there is.

Here we can see how neatly the different aspects of the *Tractatus* agree with each other and support each other. If the objects of the *Tractatus* were not phenomenological, we could not easily think of them as necessarily existing, let alone be forced to do so. Later in his philosophical life, Wittgenstein came to consider the *Tractatus* analysis of quantified propositions as his worst mistake there. But even if the reduction works, Wittgenstein still has problems on his hands. He has to show that every sentence formulated by means of the logic of logical connectives, propositional logic, can be construed as a picture. Such interpretability is highly plausible in the case of unanalyzable (elementary, atomic) propositions, but can it be extended to all sentences of propositional language? Wittgenstein studies this logic in the *Tractatus*, showing that propositional logic can be interpreted as the logic of truth-functions, in other words, that the meaning of its logical constants is defined by the way the truth-value (*true* or *false*) of a complex expression depends on the truth-values of its component expressions. For instance, the meaning of the conjunction "&" is determined by its "truth table" which says that (A&B) is true if and only if A and B are both true, otherwise false. Finally, Wittgenstein points out that all truth-functions can be reduced to a single one, which is the conjunction of the negations of its arguments. This truth-function is generally known as the Sheffer stroke.

So what? We have here an interpretational problem which ought to stare every reader of the *Tractatus* in the face. The problem is: What is the argumentative structure of the *Tractatus*? Its seven main propositions are:

1. The world is everything that is the case.
2. What is the case, the fact, is the existence of atomic facts.
3. The logical picture of the facts is the thought.
4. The thought is a significant proposition.
5. Propositions are truth-functions of elementary propositions.
6. The general form of truth-function is [$\bar{p}$, $\bar{\xi}$, $N(\bar{\xi})$] [that is, the Sheffer operator just explained]
7. Whereof one cannot speak, thereof one must be silent

Here, 1-4, with their accompanying propositions, present Wittgenstein's overall vision, and 7 is the moral of the story. But what is the role of 5-6, especially 6, which should be the culmination of the entire book? What do the niceties of truth-function theory have to do with Wittgenstein's overall vision?

23

The answer lies in what was said in Chapter 2 of Wittgenstein's argumentation. Wittgenstein presents his grand vision in the beginning of the book, including the picture theory. Propositions from 4.1 on are in effect part of Wittgenstein's conclusion from his overall theory or, in the light of Wittgenstein's metatheoretical self-denial, non-theory). But the definitive arguments for the picture theory come only later. As was pointed out, Wittgenstein can take the picture idea to be fairly obvious in the case of elementary ("atomic") propositions. But he has to extend it to all truth functions of elementary propositions which he thinks exhaust our language. But how does the Sheffer stroke idea help him? Conjunction has a pictorial meaning. A conjunction of pictures is simply a composite picture. But how can the negation ~S of a prepositional "picture" S be a picture? Easily, Wittgenstein thinks. It is the same picture as S, but taken with the opposite sense (in the Tractarian sense of "sense"). (S and ~S are like the positive and the negative of the same snapshot.) In this way, the Sheffer stroke representation puts the finishing touches to Wittgenstein's argument for the picture theory. In this sense, proposition 6 is, not the culmination of Wittgenstein's argument, but the step that fills the last gap in his argument.

The most remarkable thing about Wittgenstein's picture theory is not that he thought of it as the truth and nothing but the truth, but that it was for him the whole truth about language and the way it works. For instance, a verificatory comparison between a proposition and reality must be immediate. As Wittgenstein puts it,

> One must be able to put the proposition on the top of reality .

There cannot be any process of language-world comparisons for then the logic of these comparisons would be, not only additional to, but also more fundamental than, the pictorial logic of the *Tractatus*. This completeness presupposes the exhaustiveness of the truth-function theory. And this in turn presupposes that elementary propositions are logically independent of each other, for otherwise there must be a logic governing their mutual relations.

This independence has a remarkable consequence: If elementary propositions are logically independent of each other, all possible distributions of truth-values on them are possible. Then the only propositions that are true for purely logical reasons are disjunctions that admit all such distributions. But they do not exclude any possibilities of how things might be. They do not say anything about the world;

24

they are tautological. Conversely, if logical truths are tautological in this sense, elementary propositions must be independent of each other.

Once again, it is not immediately obvious that the objects of my experience can all be described by means of a language where elementary propositions are logically independent of each other. If color attributions are such elementary propositions, they are not independent, for the statement "this point is red" excludes "this point is green," However, Wittgenstein thought at the time of the *Tractatus* that such problems can be solved by a suitable choice of a symbolism (language). In this way, Wittgenstein thought at the time he could maintain the magnificent general picture of language and reality he paints in the *Tractatus*.

But could he maintain it in the long run? The answer is that he could not. The way the structure of the *Tractatus* unraveled shows at the same time what that structure was and how Wittgenstein had to change it in order to proceed further.

5

Wittgenstein in Transition

The philosophy of the *Tractatus* could not satisfy Wittgenstein in the long run. Its weakest point turned out to be the assumption whose different but equivalent forms include the thesis of the logical independence of elementary propositions, the tautological character of logical truths and the completeness of truth-function theory as the logic of our language. The incompatibility of color attributions served Wittgenstein as a paradigm problem, even though the real issue is much more general. Whatever his reasons, he felt forced to give up this mainstay of the philosophy of the *Tractatus* and to admit that there can be logical dependencies between different elementary propositions. But what are these interconnections between elementary propositions like? In a 1929 paper, Wittgenstein tries to deal with these dependencies by assuming that elementary propositions have numerical arguments representing the dimensions of suitable spaces, for instance perceptual space or color-space. Then the logic of truth-functions will not be the basic logic of our language. A more basic "logic" is the set of arithmetical equations governing the interrelations of elementary propositions:

It seems that I am thrown back, against my will, to arithmetic.
(MS 105, p. 19)

26

One could surely replace the logic of tautologies by a logic of equations. (MS 105, p. 17)

This means that comparisons between a proposition and reality cannot any longer happen (logically speaking) at a glance. Such comparisons require certain rule-governed human activities. Soon Wittgenstein came to realize that arithmetical calculations are not the only requisite activities, but that we need operations "out there in the nature" among the object that the proposition pertains to. What happens to the picture theory? The question is not entirely sharp. The real problem is not whether propositions in some sense can be thought of as pictures. The question is how they are connected with reality. In the *Tractatus*, the language-world ties were fixed name-object relations. Now those very relations are, according to Wittgenstein's new view, constituted and maintained by certain rule-governed human activities that might perhaps be called "customs" or "institutions."

In this way, Wittgenstein could also treat the meaning of uses of language other than the fact-stating one, such as commanding and obeying. Thus his linguistic horizon was dramatically widened. But this new interest in non-descriptive use of language is not the leading new insight on the part of Wittgenstein. It was a pleasant bonus of his new position. On the contrary, the true novelty of his views is that even the descriptive meaning of our propositions has to be constituted by rule-governed activities.

But before Wittgenstein could develop these ideas further, there had to be another change in his views. The language assumed in the *Tractatus* was a phenomenological one. The objects referred to by its names were objects of immediate experience. This idea was not immediately abandoned by Wittgenstein. Not surprisingly, it became difficult for him to see that objects of immediate experience could be at the receiving end of such mediated language-world relations:

> It is as if the phenomenological language led one into a bewitched swamp where everything tangible disappears.
> (MS 105, p. 116)

Nevertheless, he thought that

> ... yet there can be a phenomenological language
> (MS 107, p. 3)

But problems accumulated. In October, 1929, Wittgenstein made a new attempt to understand the elusive "problem of truth." A

27

mediated verification activity is like a search. In such a search, I must have in mind a picture-like representation of what I am searching for. But what elements of immediate experience can there be waiting for me to discover them? Colors, for instance? But are colors objects one can look for? Does it make any sense to look for a certain color? Wittgenstein becomes more and more frustrated. On October 11, 1929, he realizes that he has been on a wrong track:

> The immediately given is in a state of constant flux. (It is like a river.)
>
> . . .
>
> It is clear that if one wants to say the last word here one must come directly to the limit of the language that expresses it.

Wittgenstein is in fact turning his line of thought around. The next thing he tries is to assert for the first time the primacy of a physicalistic everyday language over a phenomenological one:

> The worst philosophical mistakes come always about when one wants to apply our usual — physical — language in the field of the immediately given.

This leads Wittgenstein into the problem as to how experienced fuzziness is to be represented. He thinks about it for more than a week. On October 22, 1929, he is ready to draw the conclusion:

> The assumption that a phenomenological language were possible and that only it would express what we want to express is — I believe — absurd.

Hence one of the main cornerstones of the philosophy of the *Tractatus* collapsed the same week as the Wall Street.

It might not seem a big deal whether we want to speak about the world in a phenomenological or an everyday physicalistic language. However, for Wittgenstein, this change implies a radical change in his philosophical aims and in his methods of pursuing those ends. It is often thought and said that he changed his entire approach from the construction of an ideal logical language to the description of how our language in fact works. This is by and large accurate, but it was not a spontaneous, deliberate choice by Wittgenstein. He was forced to do so by his rejection of the possibility of phenomenological languages. The first book-length work Wittgenstein dictated after his return to Cambridge and after his main changes in his philosophical position in the book was published in 1964 under the title *Philosophische Bemerkungen* (*Philosophical Remarks*). If we rely upon the

28

interpretational strategy suggested in Chapter 2, then the leading ideas of this work must be found in its very beginning. Thus the reason why Wittgenstein did not after October 22, 1929, try to construct a sharp logical language is not in the first place that the world is so unsharp that we cannot capture it by an explicit language and sharp rules — even if he might have thought that this is the case. The real reason is a different one. The reality we would like to represent is a phenomenological one, but the way our language works, it can only represent directly a physical reality. This is connected with Wittgenstein's belief that

> The language itself belongs in the second [i.e., physical] system. If I describe a language, I am essentially describing something that belongs to physics. But how can a physical language describe the phenomena? (*Phil. Remarks* VII, sec. 68)

This question occupied Wittgenstein for the rest of his philosophical life. It is the converse of Russell's project of a "reduction to acquaintance." Wittgenstein's project is a reduction from the language of acquaintance to an everyday physicalistic language. The only short general answer to Wittgenstein's question is: indirectly, by various indirect means.

We can thus see how the central problems of Wittgenstein's later philosophy grew organically although not painlessly from his earlier position. It is therefore not surprising that when Wittgenstein outlined the basic ideas of his later philosophy on the thirty-some first pages of the *Philosophical Investigations*, he did it by comparing and contrasting them to the ideas he had held in the *Tractatus*. The views which he there attributes to Augustine and to other folk and then rejects are in fact a good representation of the philosophy of the *Tractatus*.

One remarkable thing about Wittgenstein's change of mind in October, 1929, is that he does not change his idea about what the reality is ultimately like that is represented in language. It still remains phenomenological for him:

> The world we live in is the world of sense-data [i.e., more generally speaking, of phenomenological objects — J. H.]; but the world we talk about is the world of physical objects. (*Wittgenstein's Lectures, Cambridge 1930-32*, p. 82)
>
> Sense-data are the source of our concepts. (*ibid.* p. 81)

There is a sense in which Wittgenstein remained a phenomenological philosopher to the end of his life. Of course, there could not according to Wittgenstein be a doctrine called "phenomenology." But the reality we have to cope with is that of objects we are acquainted with. Moreover, just as in the *Tractatus*, the phenomenological structure of the world determines its basic logic:

> Physics wants to determine regularities; it does not set its sights on what is possible. . . . In phenomenology, it is always a matter of possibility, i.e., of sense, not of truth and falsity. (*Ludwig Wittgenstein and the Vienna Circle*, p. 63)

6

A Rule of Rules?

Wittgenstein's new vision was that rule-governed human activities, not static naming relations, are the mediators of meaning. Since the objects that language is used to speak about have to persist during such activities, they can only be physical objects. Names are not like labels stuck to objects, like street numbers on houses. They get their meaning only from various activities in which they play a role. (Street numbers are useful in finding the house we are looking for.)

What are the relevant rule-governed activities like? Wittgenstein hit upon an analogy that served him well but whose role changed in the course of his development. In order to highlight the rule-governed character of language, he compares it with a game:

> When we study language we envisage it as a game with fixed rules. We compare it with an measure it against a game of that kind (*Philosophical Grammar* III, sec. 77)

This is the origin of one of the most famous concepts of Wittgenstein's later philosophy, the concept of a "language-game." It is an extremely fruitful concept which can be put to important uses, not all of which would have been approved by Wittgenstein. He claimed that this concept does not have sharp boundaries:

31

> For how is the concept of game bounded? What still counts as
> a game and what no longer does? Can you give the
> boundary? No. You can draw one; but none has so far been
> drawn. (*Philosophical Investigations* I, sec. 681)

In this case, Wittgenstein was nevertheless wrong. Apart from the ambiguities due to the double role of the German word *Spiel* as meaning either game or play, the central uses of the concept of game have so much shared structure that mathematicians like von Neumann and John Nash have constructed a detailed general theory of games which has helped scientists and philosophers to understand a range of interesting problems. They even include the problems of truth and meaning (and other language-world relations) for the discussion of which Wittgenstein introduced his notion of language-game. It may be the case that focusing on this characteristic structure amounts to a departure from our ordinary usage. But this does not affect my objection, for the usefulness of Wittgenstein's game metaphor may very well turn out to depend on the very structure that is regimented in game theory. It is therefore difficult to decide whether his notion of language-game was a serendipitous figure of speech or a brilliant intuition.

In either case, the notion of a language-game did not at first play a major role in Wittgenstein's thinking — to self-apply a metaphor. Originally, the notion only served to highlight the all-important role of rules in Wittgenstein's thinking. In the *Philosophical Grammar* II, p. 244, he goes as far as to tell his reader:

> You can't get behind rules, because there isn't any behind.

The notion of rule has a close relative in the concept of criterion. For it is clearly impossible to speak of correctly following a rule unless there are criteria of correctness. The fortunes of the two notions are in fact closely interrelated in Wittgenstein.

Gradually Wittgenstein came to realize that games are not only instructive objects of comparison; they can be instructive models for language itself, meaning of course language as it is actually used. Languages become conglomerations of language-games:

> I shall also call the whole, consisting of language and the
> activities into which it is woven the "language-game."
> (*Philosophical Investigations* I, sec. 7)

Language-games are hence not games of speaking. Their moves are not speech acts or other language acts, but typically activities

32

serving some non-linguistic purpose. Most importantly, language-games constitute the basic language-world connections.

In the end, language-games, not rules, become the last court of appeal in logic and semantics:

> Our mistake is to look for an explanation where we ought to look at what happens as a "proto-phenomenon." That is, where we ought to have said: *This language-game is being played.* (*Philosophical Investigations* I, sec. 654)

A great deal had to happen, however, before language-games could dominate over rules in Wittgenstein's thought. The first item on Wittgenstein's agenda in this direction was to understand better the ideas of rule and rule-following. In the *Blue Book*, pp. 12-13, Wittgenstein asks what happens when someone is taught the meaning of a word, that is, a rule for the usage of the word:

> . . . this teaching can be looked at in two different ways.
>
> A. The teaching is a drill. . .
>
> B. The teaching may have supplied us with a rule which is itself involved in the process of understanding, obeying, etc., "involved," however, meaning that the expression of this rule forms a part of these processes.

The reason why we have to distinguish these two cases is that

> We must distinguish between what one might call "a process being *in accordance with* a rule," and "a process involving a rule" . . . We shall say that the rule is *involved* in the understanding, obeying, etc., if, as I should like to express it, the symbol of the rules forms part of the calculation.

But what does it mean for the symbolic expression of a rule to play a part in the process of following the rule? The actual expression of the rule must guide my rule-following activity. But what does it mean to be guided by a rule? This question became one of the most important, possibly the most important problem, for Wittgenstein in his later philosophy. Among other occasions, he discusses it in a central part of the *Philosophical Investigations*, viz., Part I, secs. 143-242, known as Wittgenstein's rule-following discussion.

It can already be seen that this designation is not accurate. The problem is not what it means to follow a rule as much as it is what it is to be guided by a rule. The rule-following discussion has been given a skeptical interpretation by Robert Fogelin and later by Saul Kripke.

According to this interpretation, Wittgenstein is asking whether one can know what rule one is following and whether one is following it correctly. Careful reading of the rule-following discussion nevertheless shows what Wittgenstein's problem is and what it is not. But if Wittgenstein's rule-following discussion is not an exercise in skepticism, what is it? Here an awareness of Wittgenstein's psychological makeup provides an instructive perspective. As was seen, Wittgenstein was dyslexic. Now, a characteristic feature of many cases of dyslexia is an inability of a person to recognize the rule he or she is following. For instance, if you ask such a dyslexic: "Which way do you write the letter E, so as to open to the left or to the right?," the subject may be unable to answer even when he or she uniformly writes the letter correctly. Such a dyslexic does not know what rule he or she is following. In such cases, a dyslexic follows a rule blindly, one might say.

That one cannot find the rule one is following merely by attending to what one is doing was for Wittgenstein an important insight. He writes:

> Earlier I thought at one time that grammatical rules are an explication of what I experience on *one* occasion when I once use the word. They are according to this view as it were consequences or expressions of the properties which I momentarily experience when I understand the word. (MS 116, von Wright)

Even though Wittgenstein is here focusing on the impossibility of finding any phenomenological entity called "the rule" that guides his activity, his problem is not merely a corollary to his rejection of phenomenological languages. He is not concerned with the difference between internal and external.

I believe that Wittgenstein's problem about rule-following is less like a skeptic's worry whether she is following a rule correctly than it is like a dyslexic's puzzle as to what the rules is that she is acting in accordance with. Speaking of Wittgenstein's dyslexia, it is scarcely an accident that his most fully worked-out example is reading (reading aloud), an activity which is especially likely to be affected by dyslexia. What worries Wittgenstein is nevertheless a perfectly sensible and in fact highly important philosophical problem.

The fact that Wittgenstein's philosophical problem reflects his own psychological handicap does not reflect on its significance. On the contrary, the thorn in Wittgenstein's linguistic flesh sensitized him to a problem which other thinkers had not — and still have not — sufficiently acknowledged. On the one hand, Wittgenstein had a keen eye for activities of acting in accordance with purely formal rules. He was not for nothing the originator of the phrase "logical syntax." For instance, mathematics is according to Wittgenstein a bunch of calculations carried out in accordance with strict rules. He did not believe that there are any serious difficulties about the correct following of such rules:

> Disputes do not break out (among mathematicians, say) over the question whether a rule has been obeyed or not.
> (*Philosophical Investigations* I, sec. 240)

On the other hand, Wittgenstein correctly realized that the function of such formal rules is to guide our actions and otherwise aid and abet our intercourse with reality. Such applications (uses) of language and its logic show what they really involved. For instance, when does somebody understand the universal quantifier *all*?

> Cut down all these trees!
> — But don't you understand what "*all*" means? (He left one standing.) (*Remarks on the Foundations of Mathematics* I, sec. 10)

What was difficult for Wittgenstein was to understand precisely how the formal "games" are relevant to the applications. How can those purely formal exercises guide their own applications? This is a generalization of the problem of rule-following, where the question is how a symbolic expression can guide one's acting in accordance with it.

Wittgenstein tried in different ways to solve this main problem of his, that is, to understand the way in which a rule in its symbolic formulization can guide me. After all, the formal expression of a rule is a "dead" physical or perhaps geometrical object that has to be interpreted before it can guide me. But what is the criterion of such interpretations being right?

One explanatory gambit Wittgenstein tried was to compare a rule which guides human action with a blueprint of a machine which determines how the machine works. We can speak more generally of Wittgenstein's "machine analogies" by means of which he tried to understand and to conceptualize rule-governed human activities. However, this did not really help him because we do not really understand how the blueprint determines the actions of the machine.

35

The way a machine in fact operates or does not operate is an empirical matter, not comparable even by analogy to logical necessity.

> The machine as symbolizing its action: the action of a machine — I might say at first — seems to be there in it from the start. What does that mean? — If we know the machine, everything else, that is its movement, seem to be already completely determined.
> We talk as if these parts could only move in this way, as if they could not do anything else. How is this — do we forget the possibility of their bending, breaking off, melting, and so on? Yes; in many cases we don't think of that at all. We use a machine, or the drawing of a machine, to symbolize a particular action of the machine. For instance, we give someone such a drawing and assume that he will derive the movement of the parts from it. (*Philosophical Investigations* I, sec. 193)

Hence Wittgenstein has nearly the same difficulty of understanding a machine's rule-following as he has of understanding human rule-following. He illustrates the former problem by asking rhetorically:

> Does a calculating machine *calculate*? (*Remarks on the Foundation of Mathematics* V, sec. 1)

This is not an instance of the general question "whether computers can think." Wittgenstein's question is much deeper. He is asking whether computers really compute, that is, whether their operation is determined by real mathematical necessity.

In the end, Wittgenstein failed in his epistemological struggle, it seems to me. He could not explain to himself and to others the mechanism of rule-following. Perhaps he was right. There is no single way of following a rule. But generally speaking, there are ways of showing the connection between the formal operations practiced in logic and mathematics and their applications, but they vary from one language-game to another. A good example is offered by the *tableau* methods in first-order logic. If one uses them, a deductive proof of, say, G from F is interpreted as a frustrated effort to "describe" a scenario in which F is true but G is false. Instead of an attempt to "describe" one can even say "construct," in the sense of constructing an isomorphic replica of a possible counter-example. This way of looking at deductive proofs provides precisely the link between the formal rules of logic and the applications of logic in practice that Wittgenstein was looking for but never found, not even to his own satisfaction.

A more familiar example is provided by the rules of elementary arithmetic whose uses in applications are mediated by the language-game of counting. This particular link between formal operations and their concrete practical significance was of course familiar to Wittgenstein. But although Wittgenstein was actively searching for such ways of bringing out the concrete pragmatic meaning in different cases, he did not succeed in the case of the other rules, not even formal games that mattered most to him, such as formal theorem-proving in logic and mathematics. Even when the formal rules of arithmetic were presented in a way that did not have an equally close connection with the practice of counting, for instance, when Russell reduced the rules of arithmetic to the laws of logic, Wittgenstein found them literally uninterpretable.

7

A Rule of Language-Games?

Perhaps it is here that Wittgenstein's dyslexia got the better of him. He did not in the case of any of the conceptually central language-games give an account of the role of their rules in determining their concrete model-theoretic or other interpreted meaning, an account in the same sense in which the model-building interpretation brings out the concrete meaning of the rules of logical deduction. In the end, he decided that he could not give a general account of how a rule guides my actions. In a sense, he reverted back to do alternative A which he had rejected in the *Blue Book*: We cannot say anything more about rule-following than about acting in accordance with the rule. I do not (in principle and in typical cases) rely on any explicit formulation of the rule; we follow it as it were blindly.

What this means is that, for Wittgenstein, rules and criteria lose their primacy and become conceptually speaking subordinate to language games. According to the new conception, a language game is not taught by conveying its rules to the learner. On the contrary, those rules are understood only by mastering the language game. Not only are language games the mediators of all semantic relations between language and reality; they are also the last court of appeal in language theory. Earlier, Wittgenstein warned that there is nothing behind the rules. Now he could have put his new point by saying that there is nothing behind language games. Wittgenstein uses different language this time, but his point is obvious:

> Our mistake is to look for an explanation where we ought to look at what happens as a "proto-phenomenon," that is, where we ought to have said: *this language-game is being played.*
>
> (*Philosophical Investigations* I, sec. 654)

Wittgenstein's famous "rule-following discussion" is essentially an argument for the primacy of language games and against the idea of rules guiding our behavior. The symbolic expression of one rule does not guide my behavior in following it. I follow it "blindly" as Wittgenstein put it.

But this did not absolve Wittgenstein from giving an account of how we came to follow rules and play language-games. Since one does not follow rules because one has them so to speak before one's mind's eye — and sometimes before one's physical eye — it cannot be the case that a language-game is taught to a learner by communicating its rules to him. According to Wittgenstein, a language-game is not taught by conveying its rules, but by training the learner to behave in a certain way. And this idea of training must be separated from learning in the usual intellectual sense. Wittgenstein's characteristic term for this kind of teaching is *abrichten*, a word which you could use of the training of a dog to behave in a certain way.

Wittgenstein realizes, correctly, that this kind of training does not happen word by word, for then what is learned would be a criterion for the use of the word. What the learner is trained in is playing an entire language-game.

It follows that, according to Wittgenstein, language-games are more than the mediators of the language-world relations. They are also our entry to language. Language is learned by being trained to master different language-games.

These points are illustrated by one of Wittgenstein's most famous philosophical analysis, his so-called "private language" argument. It is found in *Philosophical Investigations* I, secs. 243-317. Since it is a separate discussion of a problem or problem areas, we can expect to be able to use the interpretational idea presented in Chapter 2 above. Among other things, we can expect Wittgenstein to state his main ideas in the beginning of the discussion. This he in fact does. In *Philosophical Investigations* I, secs. 243-244, he writes:

A human being can encourage himself, give himself orders,
obey, blame and punish himself; he can ask himself a question
and answer it. We could even imagine human beings who
spoke only in monologue; who accompanied their activities by
talking to themselves. — An explorer who watched them and
listened to their talk might succeed in translating their
language into ours. (This would enable him to predict these
people's actions correctly, for he also hears them making
resolutions and decisions.) (*Philosophical Investigations* I,
sec. 243)

How do words *refer* to sensations? — There doesn't seem to
be any problem here; don't we talk about sensations every
day, and give them names? But how is the connexion
between the name and the thing named set up? This question
is the same as: how does a human being learn the meaning of
the names of sensations? — of the word "pain" for example.
(*Philosophical Investigations* I, sec. 244)

Here you see Wittgenstein putting his cards on the table. The
most remarkable thing here is that we can see clearly what Wittgenstein
is not doing. He is not denying the reality of inner experience, either
my own or another person's. He is not doubting the expressibility of
one's feelings and sensations, either. His question is: How do we
manage to express them? This is indeed a genuine problem for
Wittgenstein. According to him, all meaning is mediated by public
language-games. But there apparently are no language-games where
private experiences could play a role. Just because we are talking
about private experience, there cannot be any other person looking
over my shoulder to check whether I am referring to my sensations
correctly. Since I am the only person who has access to my inner
experience, I alone can refer to them — or at least I can do so without
the benefit of any external criteria. This would violate Wittgenstein's
idea that all meaning and all reference is constituted and mediated by
language-games.

Hence, Wittgenstein's problem is not whether private experiences
are real or whether we can speak of them, but what language-games
can serve the purpose. But do we really need language-games in this
case? Wittgenstein has to deny the possibility of a private language
because its possibility would be a counter-example to his thesis of the

universal role of language games as mediators of meaning. Hence his
question becomes:

> But could we also imagine a language in which a person could
> write down or give vocal expression to his inner experiences
> — his feelings, moods, and the rest — for his private use? —
> Well, can't we do so in our ordinary language? — But that is
> not what I mean. The individual words of this language are to
> refer to what can only be known to the person speaking; to his
> immediate private sensations. So another person cannot
> understand the language. (*Philosophical Investigations* I,
> sec 243)

But how can such a private language operate?

> The question is the same as: how does a human being learn
> the meaning of the names of sensations? — of the word "pain"
> for example. Here is one possibility: words are connected
> with the primitive, the natural, expressions of the sensation
> and used in their place. A child has hurt himself and he cries;
> and then adults talk to him and teach him exclamations and,
> later, sentences. They teach the child new pain-behaviour.
> (*Philosophical Investigations* I, sec. 244)

In other words, one language game that can give our pain
vocabulary its meaning involves spontaneous expressions of pain.
Indeed, verbal expressions of pain are an acquired mode of pain
behavior:

> "So you are saying that the word 'pain' really means crying?"
> — On the contrary: the verbal expression of pain replaces
> crying and does not describe it.(*Philosophical Investigations* I,
> sec. 244)

Wittgenstein's point could be seen more clearly if he had allowed
us the counterlogical thought-experiment of private language. The
problem could then be to correlate these idiosyncratic idioms so as to
merge them into our public language. Then it becomes obvious that
such an interpretation of private language can only take place with the
help of some publicly available framework. The use which the
speakers would have to make of this framework could constitute the
apparently missing language-game.

Even though such thought-experiments would violate what is
possible according to Wittgenstein, he comes close to such a scenario
in *Philosophical Investigations* I, sec. 293:

Now someone tells me that *he* knows what pain is only from his own case! — Suppose everyone had a box with something in it: we call it a "beetle." No one can look into anyone else's box, and everyone says he knows what a beetle is only by looking at *his* beetle. — Here it would be quite possible for everyone to have something different in his box. One might even imagine such a thing constantly changing. — But suppose the word "beetle" had a use in these people's language? — If so it would not be used as the designation [*Bezeichnung*] of a thing. The thing in the box has no place in the language-game at all; not even as a *something*: for the box might even be empty. — No, one can 'divide through' by the thing in the box; it cancels out, whatever it is.

Wittgenstein's thesis becomes clear when we realize that by "name" and "naming" (German: *Name* and *benennen*), Wittgenstein means any way in which an expression can represent reality whereas by "designation" and "designate" (German: *Bezeichnung* and *bezeichnen),* he means an alleged direct reference not mediated by any language-game. It is especially important to realize that Wittgenstein does not mean by the last quoted sentence that the private object (private experience) does not in fact play any role in the language. On the contrary, Wittgenstein is saying that it is irrelevant only on the mistaken assumption that words like "beetle" could operate as mere designations independent of any language-game. Indeed, the quoted passage continues as follows:

> That is to say: if we construe the grammar of the expression of sensation on the model of 'object and designation' the object drops out of consideration as irrelevant. (*Philosophical Investigations* I, sec. 293)

For instance, Wittgenstein's beetle people could happily discuss the colors of their respective beetles as long as the meaning of their color terms is established by reference to mutually available color use, e.g., public color samples. In general, we can speak in language of private objects, but only by reference to a public framework.

Private languages are according to Wittgenstein impossible only in the sense of languages not constituted by any language-game. Private experiences are likewise eminently real. That we can speak of them only with the help of a public language-game does not set them apart from the rest of reality.

Unfortunately, Wittgenstein's point is obscured in the English translation by the translator's failure to grasp the precise meaning of Wittgenstein's words; in fact, the crucial distinction between name and designation is lost in the English version.

Wittgenstein's private language argument shows several important things about language-games more generally. For one thing, we can now see what Wittgenstein means by private language. It is not contrasted by him to public languages in a societal sense of public. What Wittgenstein means by public as distinguished from private is what is publicly accessible. Likewise, what Wittgenstein calls private is what is not accessible to other people, not what is not shared by a community. The reason for the public character of language in this sense is the reliance of all language on language-games. At the interface of language and the world, the activities involved are especially carried out in physical space among physical and other public objects. Indeed, it is the game-like character of language use that makes language essentially public, according to Wittgenstein.

> The conception of solipsism does not extend to games.
> Another person can play chess as well as I. (*Philosophical Occasions*)

That is, when we play a game, we are on the same level. But this public character of language-games does not mean that they are social phenomena. It is generally believed that Wittgenstein thought of language as an intrinsically social phenomenon. Sometimes it is thought that this is because the rules and criteria of language use must be grounded in the judgment of the language community. Now, Wittgenstein might very well have believed that language is in fact societal in nature. What Wittgenstein argues is nevertheless only that language is an essentially public enterprise in the sense of being publicly accessible. A belief in the social nature of language is not a part of Wittgenstein's argument nor implied by its conclusion. On the contrary, Wittgenstein makes it completely clear that an isolated person can have a language:

> We can imagine a Robinson [Crusoe] using a language for himself, but then he must *behave* in a certain way or we shouldn't say that he plays a language-game with himself. (MS 148, p. 24)

43

In his argumentation, Wittgenstein never evokes the idea of a language community or the need for other persons to enforce the rules of language.

According to Wittgenstein, the relation of an internal experience to its public manifestation is not epistemic, e.g., evidential, but semantic. Pain *is* what manifests itself in a certain way or, rather, a certain variety of ways. In their primary uses, attributions of pain are not subject to doubt or further inquiry. Imagine a doctor asking a nurse, "Is the patient in pain?" The nurse answers "He is moaning." The appropriate response is not to raise the question of whether the patient is really in pain or merely exhibiting a certain kind of behavior. The next move in the "language-game" is likely to be to try to help the poor man. As Wittgenstein puts it,

> For how can I even try to use language to get between pain
> and its expression? (*Philosophical Investigations* I, sec. 245)

At the same time, it is seen that there must be more to our vocabulary and semantics for internal experiences. For sometimes we can drive a wedge between pain and pain expression, for instance when we say that someone is only pretending to be in pain. Does this show that Wittgenstein is wrong? No, what it shows is that there are further language-games in which an expression for pain no longer operates as a form of pain behavior. Wittgenstein assumes that such language-games are secondary with respect to the kind of game which operates by means of spontaneous pain expressions. One sign of this difference is that such secondary language-games have to be learned separately. For instance,

> Lying is a language-game that needs to be learned like any
> other one. (*Philosophical Investigations* I, sec. 249)

> Why can't a dog simulate pain? Is he too honest?
> (*ibid.* sec. 250)

In trying to determine in a concrete situation whether a person is really in pain or only exhibiting pain behavior, we are not using a person's behavior only as evidence of his inner state. We are using it also as a clue to the question as to what kind of language-game is being played. If I came upon a man lying in the street and moaning, I am likely to rush to help him. But I may also look around me to see whether I might have unwittingly come upon a scene in a movie that is being filmed or perhaps whether I can spot the candid camera.

In general, we have to distinguish primary language-games from secondary ones that are parasitic on them. (There cannot be lying without truth-telling.) Wittgenstein's strong (and in my judgment ultimately dubious) thesis seems to be that all primary language-games operate in principle by means of immediate inculcated responses, just like our pain discourse. This he asserts in so many words about our color concepts:

> I treat color concepts like the concepts of sensation. (*Remarks on Color* III, sec. 71)

This applies even more widely:

> I look at an animal and am asked: "What do you see?" I answer: "A rabbit." — I see a landscape; suddenly a rabbit runs past. I exclaim: "A rabbit!"

> Both things, both the report and the exclamation, are expressions of perception and of visual experience. But the exclamation is so in a different sense from the report: it is forced from us. — It is related to the experience as a cry is to pain. (*Philosophical Investigations* II, p. 197)

One might describe Wittgenstein's idea here as an analogue to the *Tractatus'* doctrine of the possibility (and necessity) of immediate confrontation of a proposition and reality. Instead of a proposition, it is now an entire primary language-game that has an immediate relation to reality. Wittgenstein believes that such a direct relationships is necessary for our language to have its meaning:

> It is nonsense to say: the expression can always lie. The language games with expressions of feelings are based on games with expressions of which we don't say how they may lie. (*Philosophical Occasions*, p. 245)

It is far from clear, however, that Wittgenstein is right in thinking that at the bottom of all our language there are primary language-games which operate via spontaneous reactions to different experiences. It is for instance known that our color judgments do not depend on immediate responses to light of different wavelengths but also on comparisons of the wavelength of the light emitted from a certain part of the visual field and the wavelengths of the radiation from the adjacent areas. Again, the most basic arithmetical games involve much more than merely being able to recite the multiplication table.

Wittgenstein does not highlight the distinction between primary and secondary language-games. For instance, he does not ordinarily use the words "primary" and "secondary." The distinction is nevertheless vital for his thinking. For instance, the fact that according to Wittgenstein, primary language-games operate in a way which does not enable us to drive a wedge between language and its expression has remarkable consequences of his epistemology. It means that in the primary language-game, there is no room for notions like doubt, certainty, justification, criteria, knowledge, belief, disbelief, etc., that is to say, for notions that philosophers would call epistemic. This lends Wittgenstein's epistemology its characteristic flavor.

The other side of the coin is that we can use epistemic concepts in suitable secondary language-games:

> ... if I assume the abrogation of the normal language-game
> with the expression of a sensation, I need a criterion of
> identity for the sensation; and then the possibility of error also
> exists. (*Philosophical Investigations* I, sec. 288)

It follows that the use of epistemic concepts is always relative to some secondary language-game from which they receive their precise meaning. For instance, when a medical researcher says that he or she *knows* that an experimental vaccine is safe, the force of "knows" is not the same as when a theoretical physicist says that he or she *knows* that a new theory is true, and in neither case is it the same as when a mathematician claims to know what the solution to a mathematical problem is. This makes it very hard to say anything about knowledge in general in Wittgensteinian terms. What we can understand better is his methodology. One of the most characteristic turns in Wittgenstein's philosophical argumentation is to ask: When would we seriously say so? And what would the point of saying so be? For instance, when would we seriously say, "I know my own name" or "I know that that is a tree"? Since Wittgenstein held that the meaning of a word can in typical cases be identified with its use, it is often thought that by raising such questions, Wittgenstein was trying to get at the use of such key words as "know." It cannot be said that he was not, but that is not the whole story. A word cannot be understood apart from the ways it can be combined with other words into sentences. Utterances of sentences cannot in turn be understood without understanding the language game in which it is a move. But understanding a language game involves understanding the purpose it serves. Hence in a sense questions of use will ultimately pertain to the nature and even the purpose of an entire language-game. For instance, one might say (as Wittgenstein does) that our language-game with names is in fact such that knowing one's own name is the most certain thing. Thus, typically, Wittgenstein's questions like: "When would we ever say that?" are calculated to call attention to the language-game that is being played and its characteristics, not to the usage of some one word or phrase. What was seen earlier is that in the case of epistemic language-games, their differences are highly relevant just because epistemic notions are relative to some particular secondary language-game.

In spite of what has been said, it should not come as a surprise that there is in Wittgenstein's later philosophy a subtle but unmistakable tension between his emphasis on language-games as mediators of all meaning and his idea that all language-games are ultimately based on games operating by means of spontaneous responses. For one thing, in such language-games it is hard to find any niche for the concept of strategy, even though this concept is the most crucial one in any systematic theory of games.

For instance, even though the arithmetical calculation "games" which Wittgenstein frequently uses as examples do involve rote rules like the multiplication table, such rules do not exhaust what goes on in arithmetic. For instance, abstract rules like commutativity and associativity are also involved, and they cannot be reduced to blind rule-following.

8

The Rest of Wittgenstein

Wittgenstein worked incessantly. After his death, more than two dozen volumes of his writings have been published not to mention several volumes of notes from his lectures and half a dozen or so volumes of letters to and from him. Five volumes of so-called Wiener Ausgabe have been published, covering the notebooks numbered 105-108 in von Wright's catalogue. This still leaves a tremendous amount of material unpublished. All of it will be made available in CD-ROM form by Oxford University Press. The first CD-ROM disk appeared in 1999.

It is, nevertheless, not only the extent of Wittgenstein's philosophical writing that might prompt someone to wonder whether his philosophical ideas have been done justice to in the preceding chapters. There are in fact three different kinds of apparent omissions. First, Wittgenstein's ideas on a number of specific topics have not been discussed. Second, at least one major problem area, Wittgenstein's philosophy of mathematics, has not been covered. Third, the significance of Wittgenstein's thought for wider issues in philosophy and outside it have not been touched. These include Wittgenstein's position in the history of philosophy and his own attitude to traditional philosophy; his ideas about contemporary culture and its prospects; the relevance of his ideas for social science, for social and political issues, religion, music and the arts, all of which can perhaps be comprehended in the vague German term *Weltanschauung*. In the last two chapters, an attempt is made to correct these *prima facie* omissions.

Many of Wittgenstein's ideas can be given a relatively short shift in the light of the dialectical structure of his thought and writing described in Chapter 2 above. There it was pointed out that one of the main ways in which Wittgenstein argues for his overall ideas is to consider actual or possible objections to them and then refute the objections. The fact that there are sometimes paranoid overtones to this tactic does not matter to the evaluation of Wittgenstein's ideas. What is relevant here is that Wittgenstein's defensive maneuvers in trying to deflect criticisms are not always dictated by his central ideas or indicators of them. For instance, one of the best known Wittgensteinian locutions is "family resemblance." The idea it embodies is not a brilliant, fresh philosophical insight, however. It is a memorable metaphor calculated to illustrate Wittgenstein's attempted response to potential criticisms. Wittgenstein held, as seen in Chapter 7 above, that the conceptual primacy belongs in language to entire language-games, not to their rules or the criteria by means of which these rules operate. Now any concept which seems to operate by sharp criteria is a putative counter-example to such a view. As against such views, Wittgenstein had to maintain that typically our words do not operate by any shared defining properties but by means of a network of partial similarities comparable to family resemblances which do not mean sharing any one particular characteristic.

But even if Wittgenstein is right in suggesting that our concepts do not in the last analysis rely on shared properties, his claim will not help him very much. For there are other ways in which the different uses of a concept can be related to each other in a sharp definable way. For instance, it is not hard to appreciate the fact that many of our most important concepts, arguably including the concept of a physical object, operate essentially by means of continuity. Wittgenstein at one point asks himself in effect what justifies one to say things like "This is not the same chair as was here yesterday, even though it is precisely similar." The answer is of course that in order to be the same, the chairs must be stages of one and the same life history of the piece of furniture in question. Moreover, questions of continuity in the relevant sense are subject to explicit mathematical treatment. Hence, the notion of family resemblance has little value as a tool of conceptual analysis or as an indication of Wittgenstein's central ideas.

A somewhat more interesting case is affected by what Wittgenstein calls "aspect seeing." In the *Tractatus*, Wittgenstein had used the well-known ambiguous figured called the "Necker cube" to illustrate his ideas. This schematic figure can be seen in two different ways, either as having a different facet in front. In the context of the *Tractatus*, this was a brilliant example in support of his views. In physicalistic terms, there is only one set of objects and one set of relations between them. Yet one can see two different configurations there. Hence what one sees cannot be a configuration of physical objects; the objects we speak about must be phenomenological, objects of my visual experience.

This was fine and dandy for Wittgenstein's purposes until he changed his idea of our actual basic language, which now became physicalistic rather then phenomenological. (See Chapter 5 above.) What this means is that ambiguous configurations like the Necker cube became *prima facie* counter-examples to his post-October 1929 views.

Hence, Wittgenstein did not discuss this problem in his later philosophy — for instance in the *Philosophical Investigations* II xi, pp 193-215 — because he thought that he had found a new philosophically interesting problem or insight but because he had to do so in order to defend his own views against objections.

It is true that the problem in question is a fascinating one. Wittgenstein called the different things one can see in a Necker cube or in some other ambiguous figure "aspects" and called the problem he was dealing with "the problem of aspect seeing." It is interesting to note that the word "aspect" (or, rather, its German cognate *Aspekt*) has in Wittgenstein's usage a close relationship to the notion of a phenomenological object. At one point he calls what is referred to by "this" and "that" aspects.

Once Wittgenstein realized the interest of the problem of aspect seeing, he analyzed it far beyond his mere defensive needs. However, the details of his discussion receive their interest largely from their connection with his overall theories. The problem is not any longer a monopoly of Wittgenstein's, either (if it ever was). The phenomenon of aspect seeing has to be dealt with in any satisfactory logical analysis of our perceptual language. And it is not clear that Wittgenstein's informal, impressionistic approach is the best one in this direction.

Similar things can be said of Wittgenstein's discussions of several other specific problems. But what is then to be said of Wittgenstein's philosophy of mathematics? His comments on mathematics are at first sight probably the most surprising he ever made. They are also the most controversial. Some admirers have professed to find nuggets of deep wisdom in them, whereas other commentators have dismissed them as nonsense. For instance, Wittgenstein's approach to mathematics was singularly out of step with the others at the time because of his deepseated conviction that one cannot speak in any language about the semantics of that language, that is, about its relationships to reality. In contemporary logicians' jargon, this made any idea of model theory an anathema for him, for the very idea of model theory is to study the different interpretations of a logical or mathematical language. In particular, any attempt to apply logic or mathematics to study itself, that is, any idea of metamathematics, was considered absurd by Wittgenstein. How alienated this made him from the rest of logical and foundational studies can perhaps be gauged by the fact that the original leading idea of contemporary logic was to use mathematical methods to study logical and mathematical reasoning. Thus, Wittgenstein totally rejected Hilbert's metamathematics and the self-referential methods Gödel used in his famous incompleteness proofs.

Wittgenstein's comments on logic and mathematics during his later period do not show that he had much of a grasp of what mathematicians and logicians were doing. Not surprisingly, these comments are not helpful for anybody actually working in these areas. In spite of this, Wittgenstein's struggles with the foundations of mathematics are of great interest. His genius shows up even in areas that he had least sympathy with or understanding of.

Wittgenstein's main problem in trying to understand logical and mathematical reasoning can be formulated in his own terms. What are the language-games that are the "logical home" of mathematical and logical concepts? Wittgenstein was keenly interested in formal "games" with mathematical concepts. In the simplest possible terms, mathematics was for the mature Wittgenstein a collection of calculi or "systems." All such calculi are on the same level. Not only is it the case that a logical or mathematical system cannot be self-applied; one mathematical calculus cannot say anything about others. For instance, logical inferences are purely formal operations:

What we call "logical inference" is a transformation of our expression. For instance, the translation of one measure into another. (*Remarks on the Foundations of Mathematics* I, sec. 9)

The same holds of the meaning of logical words:

One learns the meaning of "all" by learning that "fa" follows from "(x)fx" (*ibid.* sec. 10)

Likewise, mathematical truth is defined by such formal games:

For what does a proposition's "*being true*" mean? "p" is true = p. . . So we want to ask something like: under what circumstances do we assert a proposition? . . . If, then we ask in this sense: "Under what circumstances is a proposition asserted in Russell's game?" the answer is: at the end of his proofs, or as a "fundamental law" . . . (*Remarks on the Foundations of Mathematics* I, appendix iii, sec. 6)

But these formal games cannot be the only ones played with mathematical and logical words. For there are such things as applications of logic and mathematics in practice. Wittgenstein had a keen sense of such applications. For:

What I want to say: it is essential to mathematics that its signs are also employed *in mufti*. It is the use outside mathematics and hence the *meaning* of signs that makes the sign game into mathematics. (*Op. cit.* V, sec. 2)

What is that "civilian life" of logical words like? Wittgenstein gives an example:

Cut down all these trees! — But don't you understand what "*all*" means? (He had left one standing.) (*Op. cit.* I, sec. 10)

But which kind of game, formal or applied, is the one that primarily gives logical and mathematical words their meaning? How is it that the formal operations of a calculus with these words pertain to their role in applications? Wittgenstein does not answer these questions, the reason being that he never could grasp the relationship between the two kinds of "games." Here it is hard not to suspect that this problem was made especially hard for Wittgenstein by his dyslexia. Dyslexics of the kind Wittgenstein was find it difficult to master intellectually complex structures when they are presented verbally or otherwise symbolically, as distinguished for instance from a geometrical representation.   It is instructive to note that Wittgenstein found it much easier to understand geometrical than logical necessity:

> Logic as the foundation of mathematics does not work, and to show this it is enough that the cogency of logical proof stands and falls with its geometrical cogency. (*Op. cit.* III, sec. 43)

Likewise, in his discussion of Gödel's results, Wittgenstein says that he can understand how a geometrical proposition can apply to itself (as a structure of scratches on a paper), but he cannot understand how an arithmetical proposition can do so.

Wittgenstein's failure to solve what might be called "the problem of the interpretation of logic" might not seem to be his credit.   He struggled with the problem, but in the end did not come up with many constructive insights.   Yet what Wittgenstein did was remarkable in two different ways: First, the interpretation problem — or task — is a very real one.   Yet it was and still is neglected, greatly to the detriment of the philosophy of logic and mathematics.   For instance, what is the concrete interpretational meaning of deductive arguments?   One possible answer is the idea of the simplest deductive arguments as frustrated counter-model constructions implicit in the logical proof methods known as the tree method or *tableau* methods.   Such interpretation would have been at least partial answers to Wittgenstein's prayers.   Yet, their full significance has not been spelled out.   And many other possibilities of interpretations have been neglected, at least until very recently.   Hence Wittgenstein's main concern in the philosophy of mathematics is of a tremendous interest and importance.

As was indicated, Wittgenstein himself never solved his own main problem nor even contributed very much to its solution.   This makes his remarks on the foundations of mathematics inconclusive and frequently irritating.   Yet, subjectively speaking, Wittgenstein's concern with this particular problem amounts to an impressive feat of self-knowledge.   He was able to recognize, albeit not with full clarity, what the problem was that was caused by his dyslexia and to realize its general importance.

53

9

Logic, Sins and Hell

Those readers who know something about Wittgenstein's philosophical reputation may have been surprised by what they find in this book — or, rather, what they do not find here. Wittgenstein's thought is typically taken to have important consequences for a large number of philosophically and humanly important issues. A selection of entries from Wittgenstein's notebooks was published in English translations with the pretentious title *Culture and Value*. Books have appeared bearing such titles as *Wittgenstein: A Social Theory of knowledge* (Bloor); *Wittgenstein: A Religious Point of View* (Malcolm); *Transcendence and Wittgenstein's Tractatus* (Hodges); *Wittgenstein and Justice* (Pitkin); *Theology after Wittgenstein* (Kerr); and so on. These topics are much more closely related to the traditional great philosophical problems than the ones discussed in this book. Am I leaving out the most important and interesting part of Wittgenstein's philosophy?

The right person to answer this question is Wittgenstein himself. And the answer we got from him is unmistakable. The ideas and their expressions that are examined in this book are the ones Ludwig Wittgenstein spent most of his adult life working on with an intensity that is not often — if ever — matched by any thinker. They are his life work. Any construal of his philosophy in general must be based in an interpretation of this hard core of his thought.

Furthermore, the relationships of Wittgenstein's thought to the views and doctrines of other philosophers are so ambivalent that they have to be approached with caution. For instance, one influential tradition maintains that Wittgenstein's thought is quite foreign to that of the members of the group of logical positivists called the "Vienna Circle." Yet Wittgenstein's own testimony tells a different story. When one of the leading members of the Vienna Circle, Rudolf Carnap, sent an offprint of his latest paper to Wittgenstein in the spring of 1932, Wittgenstein flew into a rage and accused Carnap, not of criticizing or misunderstanding his, Wittgenstein's, ideas, but of stealing them — or at least of using them without acknowledgment and without permission. In view of Wittgenstein's 1929 conversion from phenomenological to physicalistic languages, it should not be surprising that the most important allegedly stolen idea was the primacy of physicalistic language. When Carnap in response denied having heard Wittgenstein expounding the new ideas or finding them in *Tractatus*, Wittgenstein responded by accusing Carnap of plagiarizing his earlier work, too.

Likewise, it has been suggested and argued that Wittgenstein was waging a systematic campaign against traditional philosophy designed to rid our thinking of all metaphysical ideas. It is true that Wittgenstein thought of typical philosophical problems as being due to confusion and that he had a very low opinion of the intellectual level of most contemporary philosophical writing. To Norman Malcolm, Wittgenstein compared the leading British philosophy journal *Mind* unfavorably to American pulp detective magazines. But he was struggling far too intensively with his own problems to care much about other philosophers' confusions and mistakes, let alone to be engaged in a systematic campaign against them. Wittgenstein rejected many traditional philosophical problems and views, which makes it dangerous to discuss his philosophy by reference to them. For instance, it does not say anything of Wittgenstein's philosophy of mathematics to say that he rejected Platonism in mathematics. His own thought was problem-oriented, and he was keenly aware of the difficulty of these problems. One of the statements of Russell's that Wittgenstein especially liked was the exclamation "Logic is hell!"

As was indicated, Wittgenstein made comments on a rich variety of subjects of general philosophical and human interest. It is impossible to present an overview of his pronouncements on such matters. But if they are supposed to be part and parcel of his philosophical thought or at least based on it, it is in order to try to see their connection to Wittgenstein's theoretical ideas.

Or is there such a connection? Are Wittgenstein's pronouncements on ethics, culture, music, art and life perhaps mere *obiter dicta*, without any deeper connection with his theoretical thought? An answer is again given by Wittgenstein himself, however indirectly. Bertrand Russell tells of finding Wittgenstein in a brooding mood and asking him whether he was thinking of logic or of his sins. Wittgenstein answered, "Both." Russell's mocking story shows that he missed the key to the unity of Wittgenstein's thought. Wittgenstein could think of logic and ethics at the same time because to him language and its logic were a simile for life, prominently including the ethical principles we need to conduct our life. Or perhaps one can say even more. Language was for him a test case for our ethical life. Here Wittgenstein's way of thinking resembles closely that of his Viennese neighbor and older contemporary Karl Kraus (1874-1936). Wittgenstein listed in fact Kraus among the people who had influenced him most strongly, even though he did not befriend Kraus and even though it is hard to find any specific traces of Kraus' influence in Wittgenstein's philosophical writings. What is common to Kraus and Wittgenstein is their attitude to language. For Wittgenstein in the *Tractatus* philosophy is literally "critique of language." Likewise, Kraus' weapon in his practical and ideological fight was a merciless analysis of his opponents' language:

> Kraus's satire has from the first to last a linguistic basis. . . .
> An exceptional sensitivity to linguistic symptoms inspires his
> critique of the hollow rhetoric of public affairs prior to 1914.
> And during the war itself he emerged as the first great critic of
> propaganda, anticipating Orwell's vision of a totalitarian
> dominated by doublethink and newspeak. (Edward Timms,
> *Karl Kraus*, Yale University Press, 1986, p. 341)

The analogy with Wittgenstein's rejection of traditional philosophy is obvious. But the deeper similarity is that in both cases the critique of language had an ethical significance. To purify one's language is to purify one's thinking. Kraus is speaking also for Wittgenstein in one of his best known aphorisms:

> What a life-style could develop if the only ordinances that the

Germans obeyed were those of language!

The same idea was expressed earlier by Lichtenberg:

> I have often . . . wished that there could be a language in which one could not even express falsehoods or [in which] an error against truth were a grammatical one.

Wittgenstein realized that one cannot rule out factual falsehoods from the language. But the language envisaged in the *Tractatus* is one from which all nonsense, all logical errors, have been eliminated. And the underlying assumption is that this entails an elimination of inauthenticities also in the ethical sense. This approach determined also the actual content of Wittgenstein's ethics. Since the only given we need in our language according to the *Tractatus* are the names of simple objects, the only thing we need to take for granted in an authentic language is the totality of objects existing in the world. Hence one of the ethical experiences *par excellence* for Wittgenstein is one of which he says:

> I believe that the best way of describing it is to say that when I have it *I wonder at the existence of the world*. (*Philosophical Occasions*, p. 41)

Another ethical experience Wittgenstein mentions is "the experience of feeling *absolutely* safe." This can be seen as the ethical consequence of that there is no necessity in the world. The only necessity there is is the logical one, and it is empty, tautological. And if this consequence of the absence of natural necessity from Wittgenstein's world seems far-fetched, it might be recalled that ethical conclusions — albeit different from Wittgenstein's — were being drawn among Viennese intellectuals from Mach's similar views.

Hence, before anyone presumes to judge Wittgenstein's ethical views or even tries to understand them fully, he or she is well advised to seek to grasp his philosophy of language. This is the enterprise undertaken in this book. When you do so, you can also begin to understand what Russell missed when he ridiculed Wittgenstein's statement that he was thinking of logic and his sins at the same time. This is also the vantage point from which Wittgenstein's views on religion, society, art, and music must ultimately be understood.

Things might seem more complicated after Wittgenstein gave up the quest for a language from which all ambiguities and other logical infelicities have been eliminated and whose syntactical forms therefore reflects its logical forms. It also might seem that Wittgenstein became more conservative in his later philosophy both ideologically and philosophically. This might seem to be reflected among other things by his avowals to the effect that in his theory of language he did not want to change anything, merely to describe or "assemble remainders," as he sometimes put it. This change of ideological heart is largely an illusion, however. When Wittgenstein actually confronted inauthentic thinking in his later philosophy— or thought that he did — he was prepared to demand radical changes. His philosophy of mathematics is the best example of this. If mathematicians followed Wittgenstein's injunctions, they would have to abandon large segments of their enterprise. For one thing, Wittgenstein saw set theory as a colossal mistake. When I wrote in an earlier paper that "set theory was a more serious sin for Wittgenstein than sodomy," I did not intend the phrase as a hyperbole but as a literal truth. It is in any case important to realize that Wittgenstein meant what he said when he said that his new philosophical methods "do the same job as the construction of a phenomenological language" (*Philosophical Remarks* I, sec. I). Yes, things are more complex in Wittgenstein's later thought, but they are not essentially different from what they were in the *Tractatus*.

Literature

In studying Wittgenstein, it is vitally important to trust only his own writings, including notes from his lectures, rather than secondary literature. In his lifetime, Wittgenstein published only one small philosophical book, the legendary *Tractatus Logico-Philosophicus*, plus a couple of short philosophical articles and reviews (see below). He also published a dictionary of German for elementary schools. He wrote extensively, and copies of some of his writings circulated among philosophers. In his will, Wittgenstein gave the control of his manuscripts to three philosophers, namely Professors Anscombe, Rhees, and von Wright. A number of volumes have since been published. Several attempts have also been made to edit his entire writings, but the only way which has succeeded is the Norwegian project which is resulting in a CD-ROM version of the entire posthumous material. Here is a list of most of Wittgenstein's published writings, with an asterisk indicating a bilingual edition:

WITTGENSTEIN'S PUBLISHED BOOKS AND PAPERS

"On logic and how not to do it." *Cambridge Review*, vol. 34, no. 853, 6 March 1913 (review of P. Coffey, *The Science of Logic*). Rpt. in *The Cambridge Mind: Ninety Years of the Cambridge Review 1897-1969*. Ed. Eric Homberger et. al. Boston: Little, Brown, 1970. 127-9.

Tractatus Logico-Philosophicus. The German text of Ludwig Wittgenstein's *Logisch-Philosophische Abhandlung* with a new translation by D.F. Pears and B.F. McGuinness and with the Introduction by Bertrand Russell. London: Routledge & Kegan, 1961.

Wittgenstein's Tractatus. A fresh translation by Daniel Kolak, with introduction and detailed notes. Belmont: Mayfield 1998.

"Some remarks on logical form." *Proceedings of the Aristotelian Society, Supplementary Volume* 9 (1929). 162-71.

Philosophical Investigations. Trans. G.E.M. Anscombe. Oxford: Blackwell, 1953.

Remarks on the Foundations of Mathematics. Ed. G.H. von Wright, Rush Rhees, and G.E.M. Anscombe. Trans. G.E.M. Anscombe. Oxford: Blackwell, 1956.

The Blue and Brown Books (Preliminary Studies for the 'Philosophical Investigations,' Generally Known as The Blue and Brown Books). Ed. Rush Rhees. Oxford: Blackwell, 1958.

Notebooks 1914-1916. 2nd ed. (1st ed. 1961) Ed. G.H. von Wright and G.E.M. Anscombe. Trans. G.E.M. Anscombe. Oxford: Blackwell, 1979.

Philosophical Remarks. Ed. Rush Rhees. Trans. Raymond Hargreaves and Roger White. Oxford: Blackwell, 1975. German text under the title *Philosophische Bemerkungen,* same editor and publisher, 1964.

Zettel. Ed. G.E.M. Anscombe and G.H. von Wright. Trans. Denis Paul and G.E.M. Anscombe. Oxford: Blackwell, 1969.

Philosophical Grammar. Ed. Rush Rhees. Trans. Anthony Kenny. Oxford: Blackwell, 1974. German text under the title *Philosophische Grammatik,* same editor and publisher, 1969.

On Certainty. Ed. G.E.M. Anscombe and G.H. von Wright. Trans. Denis Paul and G.E.M. Anscombe. Oxford: Blackwell, 1969.

Prototractatus: An Early Version of 'Tractatus Logico-Philosophicus.' Ed. B.F. McGuinness, T. Nyberg, and G.H. von Wright. With introduction by G.H. von Wright. London: Routledge & Kegan, 1971.

Remarks on Colour. Ed. and trans. G.E.M. Anscombe. Oxford: Blackwell, 1977.

Culture and Value. Ed. G.H. von Wright in collaboration with Heikki Nyman. Trans. Peter Winch. Oxford: Blackwell, 1980. The German text was published in 1977 under the title *Vermischte Bemerkungen* by Suhrkamp Verlag, Frankfurt am Main.

*Remarks on the Philosophy of Psychology. Vol. I, Ed. G.E.M. Anscombe and G.H. von Wright, trans. G.E.M. Anscombe; vol. II, G.H. von Wright and Heikki Nyman, trans. C. G. Luckhardt and M. A. E. Aue. Oxford: Blackwell, 1980.

*Letzte Schriften über die Philosophie der Psychologie (Last Writings on the Philosophy of Psychology), vol. I: Preliminary Studies for Part II of *Philosophical Investigations*. Ed. G.H. von Wright and Heikki Nyman. Trans. C.G. Luckhardt and M.A.E. Aue. Oxford: Blackwell, 1982.

Philosophical Occasions 1912-1951. Ed. James Klagge and Alfred Nordmann. Indianapolis: Hackett, 1993.

Wiener Ausgabe (Vienna Edition). Ed. Michael Nedo, vol. 1 (1994), vol. 2 (1994), vol. 3 (1995), vol. 4 (1995), vol. 5 (1996), Register zu den Bänden 1-5 (1998), Springer Verlag, Vienna. Note: These volumes have the German text only. In spite of the title "edition," and in spite of the publication's advertisement, this is nothing like a complete edition of Wittgenstein's writings or even of his posthumous material.

Denkbewegungen: Tagebücher 1930-1932, 1936-1937. Frankfurt am Main: Fischer Taschenbuch, 1999.

Wittgenstein's entire *Nachlass* is being published by Oxford University Press in CD-ROM form. The first volume appeared in 1999.

OTHER PUBLISHED WRITINGS BY WITTGENSTEIN

"Lecture on ethics." Introduction by Rush Rhees. *Philosophical Review.* 74 (1965): 3-12.

Paul Engelmann, *Letters from Ludwig Wittgenstein, With a Memoir.* Ed. B. F. McGuinness. Trans. L. Furtmüller. Oxford: Blackwell, 1967. The German text was published under the title *Ludwig Wittgenstein, Briefe understand Begegnungen*, same editor, Vienna and Munich: Oldenbourg, 1970.

"Bemerkungen über Frazers *The Golden Bough.*" With an introductory note by Rush Rhees. *Synthese.* 17 (1967): 233-53.

"Notes for lectures on 'private experience' and 'sense data.'" Ed. Rush Rhees. *Philosophical Review.* 77 (1968): 271-320. Rpt. in *The Private Language Argument.* Ed. O.R. Jones. London: Macmillan, 1971. 226-75. This publication consists of excerpts from MSS 148, 149, and 151. Omissions are not indicated by the editor and the omitted passages are sometimes fully as important as the included material.

Briefe an Ludwig Ficker. Ed. G.H. von Wright in collaboration with W. Methlagl. Salzburg: Otto Müller Verlag, 1969.

Letters to C. K. Ogden, with Comments on the English Translation of the 'Tractatus Logico-Philosophicus.' Ed. with introduction by G.H. von Wright. Oxford: Blackwell; and London: Routledge & Kegan, 1973.

*Letters to Russell, Keynes, and Moore. Ed. with an introduction by G.H. von Wright, assisted by B. F. McGuinness. Oxford: Blackwell, 1974.

A number of letters by Wittgenstein have also been published in *Wittgenstein: Sein Leben in Bildern und Texten.* Ed. Michael Nedo and Michele Ranchetti. Frankfurt am Main: Suhrkamp Verlag, 1983.

LECTURE AND DISCUSSION NOTES NOT MADE BY WITTGENSTEIN

G. E. Moore. "Wittgenstein's lectures in 1930-33." In G. E. Moore, *Philosophical Papers.* London: Allen & Unwin, 1959.

Lectures and Conversations on Aesthetics, Psychology, and Religious Belief. Compiled from the notes taken by Yorick Smythies, Rush Rhees, and James Taylor. Ed. Cyril Barrett. Berkeley and Los Angeles: California UP, 1967.

Wittgenstein's Lectures on the Foundations of Mathematics, Cambridge 1939. From the notes of R. G. Bosanquet, Norman Malcolm, Rush Rhees, and Yorick Smythies. Ed. Cora Diamond. Ithica, Cornell UP, 1976.

Wittgenstein's Lectures, Cambridge 1932-1935. From the notes of Alice Ambrose and Margaret Macdonald. Ed. Alice Ambrose. Oxford: Blackwell, 1979.

Ludwig Wittgenstein and the Vienna Circle: Conversations recorded by Friedrich Waismann. Ed. Brian McGuinness. Trans. Joachim Schulte and Brian McGuinness. Oxford: Blackwell, 1979.

Wittgenstein's Lectures, Cambridge 1930-1932. From the notes of John King and Desmond Lee. Ed. Desmond Lee. Oxford: Blackwell, 1980.

UNPUBLISHED WRITINGS BY WITTGENSTEIN.

Wittgenstein's unpublished manuscripts are referred to by their numbers in G.H. von Wright, *Wittgenstein,* Oxford: Blackwell, 1982, and by the pages in the original MSS.

All the translations from untranslated German MSS are by Jaakko Hintikka. Whenever the German text has not been published, the original German is given along with the English translation.

Wittgenstein's posthumous material is located in Trinity College, Cambridge. A microfilm of most of it was made available by the Cornell University Library in 1967.

BIOGRAPHIES

The first short biographical work on Wittgenstein was Norman Malcolm, *Ludwig Wittgenstein: A Memoir.* Oxford: Oxford UP, 1958. It also contains a previously published "Biographical Sketch" by G.H. von Wright, originally published in *The Philosophical Review* 64 (1955).

Later, two longer biographical volumes have been published in English. They are:

McGuinness, Brian. *Wittgenstein: A Life. Young Ludwig 1889-1921.* Berkeley: California UP, 1988, and

Monk, Ray. *Ludwig Wittgenstein: The Duty of a Genius.* London: Jonathan Cope, 1990.

The source book mentioned earlier, *Ludwig Wittgenstein: Sein Leben in Bildern und Texten*, ed. Michael Nedo and Michele Ranchetti, Suhrkamp, 1983, contains much interesting biographical material.

SECONDARY LITERATURE

Many of the interpretations outlined in the present book have been documented in the following two volumes:
Hintikka, Merrill B. and Hintikka Jaakko. *Investigating Wittgenstein.* Oxford: Blackwell, 1986.
Hintikka, Jaakko. *Ludwig Wittgenstein: Half-Truths and One-and-a-Half Truths* (Selected Papers, vol. 1). Dordrecht: Kluwer Academia, 1996.

The secondary literature on Wittgenstein is enormous and much of it shows little real understanding of Wittgenstein's way of thinking or of his ideas. Some of the writers personally closest to Wittgenstein, such as G.E.M. Anscombe, Norman Malcolm and Rush Rhees, apparently had an inadequate grasp of Wittgenstein's earlier ideas and of the way they gradually developed into his later position. Therefore, they are far from ideal guides to Wittgenstein's thought. Some of the best known interpretational lines of thought fail to do justice to Wittgenstein's problems and intentions. Cases in point include the interpretation of Wittgenstein as allegedly considering language as an essentially social phenomenon (Peter Winch, David Bloor, etc.), as well as Robert Fogelin's and Saul Kripke's skeptical interpretation of Wittgenstein's rule-following discussion.

In my experience, the most perceptive philosophers who have written on Wittgenstein are G.H. von Wright and David Pears. G.H. von Wright's rare writings on Wittgenstein are collected in *Wittgenstein*, Oxford: Blackwell, 1982. David Pears has published a two-volume work: *The False Prison: A Study of the Development of Wittgenstein's Philosophy* I-II, Oxford: Clarendon Press, 1987. Many of Pears' best ideas are nevertheless found in his uncollected papers, such as "The relation between Wittgenstein's picture theory of prepositions and Russell's theory of judgments," *The Philosophical Review* 86 (1977): 177-196.

Some of the less ambitious interpreters of Wittgenstein have published well-informed and useful books on him, including for instance Peter Hacker, *Wittgenstein's Place in Twentieth Century*

Philosophy, Oxford: Blackwell, 1996; Gordon Baker and Peter Hacker, *An Analytical Commentary on the Philosophical Investigations* I-II, Oxford: Blackwell 1980-1985; S. Stephen Hilmy, *The Later Wittgenstein*, Oxford: Blackwell, 1987. There are also valuable studies of special aspects of Wittgenstein's thought, for instance Joachim Schulte, *Erlebnis und Ausdruck : Wittgensteins Philosophie der Psychologie*, Munich: Philosophia Verlag, 1987, and Mathieu Marion, *Wittgenstein, Finitism and the Foundations of Mathematics*, Oxford, Clarendon Press, 1998.